LEFKADA

Travel Guide

Discovery

Your all-in-one handbook for discovering hidden gems, top attractions, relaxation hotspots, culinary delights, and up-to-date tips on the island.

By

Christopher Morrell

COPYRIGHT NOTICE

DISCLAIMER

Please note that the information contained within this document is for educational purposes only. The information contained herein has been obtained from sources believed to be reliable at the time of publication. The opinions expressed herein are subject to change without notice.

Readers acknowledge that the Author / Publisher is not engaging in rendering legal, financial or professional advice. The Publisher / Author disclaims all warranties as to the accuracy, completeness, or adequacy of such information.

The Publisher assumes no liability for errors, omissions, or inadequacies in the information contained herein or from the interpretations thereof. The publisher / Author specifically disclaims any liability from the use or application of the information contained herein or from the interpretations thereof.

TABLE OF CONTENT

Wander through the wild beauty of Lefkada, where every turn reveals a new vista and the spirit of the island calls to the adventurer in you—are you ready to lose yourself in the breathtaking landscapes of this Ionian gem?Wander through the wild beauty of Lefkada, where every turn reveals a new vista and the spirit of the island calls to the adventurer in you—are you ready to lose yourself in the breathtaking landscapes of this Ionian gem

Introduction

G reetings, fellow travelers! If you're reading this guide, you're likely captivated by the promise of Lefkada, one of Greece's most stunning Ionian Islands. Having walked its dazzling beaches, explored its quaint villages, and immersed myself in its vibrant culture, I can tell you that Lefkada is more than just a beautiful destination—it's a place where every moment feels like a postcard come to life. This guide isn't just about pointing out places to see; it's about helping you experience Lefkada in all its glory. So, let's embark on this journey together and discover the magic of this enchanting island.

Welcome to Lefkada

Welcome to Lefkada, a gem in the Ionian Sea, known for its breathtaking beaches, lush mountains, and charming villages. Unlike many islands, Lefkada is connected to mainland Greece by a floating bridge, making it uniquely accessible. The island is a tapestry of contrasting landscapes—crystal-clear turquoise waters, white sandy beaches, and green hills dotted with olive groves. Each part of Lefkada tells a story, from the bustling streets of Lefkada Town to the tranquil shores of Porto Katsiki. Whether you're here for adventure, relaxation, or a bit of both, Lefkada promises an experience that's as diverse as its scenery.

Why Visit Lefkada?

What makes Lefkada a must-visit destination on your travel list? Here are ten compelling reasons to explore this beautiful island:

World-Class Beaches: Lefkada is home to some of the most famous beaches in Greece, like Porto Katsiki and Egremni, where the waters are impossibly blue and the cliffs dramatic.

Charming Villages: Explore traditional villages like Agios Nikitas and Karya, where time seems to stand still, and local life unfolds at a leisurely pace.

Water Sports Paradise: Lefkada is a top destination for windsurfing, kitesurfing, and sailing, particularly in the Vasiliki and Nydri areas.

Spectacular Scenery: From the lush hillsides of the interior to the rugged cliffs of the west coast, Lefkada's landscapes are truly breathtaking.

Exquisite Cuisine: Enjoy fresh seafood, local specialties like lentil soup from Eglouvi, and wines produced from the island's vineyards.

Rich History and Culture: Visit ancient monasteries, Venetian-era buildings, and the Archaeological Museum of Lefkada to delve into the island's past.

Outdoor Adventures: Lefkada offers hiking trails, waterfalls like Dimosari, and opportunities to explore caves and secluded coves by boat.

Vibrant Nightlife: Lefkada Town and Nydri offer a lively nightlife scene with bars, clubs, and seaside taverns that come alive after dark.

Island Hopping: Lefkada's location makes it a perfect base for exploring nearby islands like Meganisi, Kefalonia, and Ithaca.

Festivals and Events: Experience the local culture through traditional festivals, music events, and art exhibitions that take place throughout the year.

How to Use This Guide

This guide is crafted to be your comprehensive companion as you explore Lefkada:

Detailed Addresses and Locations: Every place recommended in this guide comes with precise addresses and coordinates to help you navigate easily.

Up-to-Date Pricing Information: Keep your budget in check with current prices for accommodations, dining, and attractions.

Real-Time Directions: Use integrated Google Maps links to find your way from one highlight to another without missing a beat.

A Brief History of Lefkada

Lefkada's history is as rich and varied as its landscapes. The island has been inhabited since prehistoric times, with archaeological finds dating back to the Paleolithic era. Throughout its history, Lefkada has seen the influence of various civilizations, including the Corinthians, Romans, Byzantines, and Venetians, each leaving its mark on the island's culture and architecture. Lefkada's strategic location made it a coveted prize in the Ionian Sea, and its history is reflected in the fortresses, churches, and ruins that dot the island. Today, Lefkada's past is preserved in its museums, monasteries, and historical sites, offering a window into the island's fascinating journey through time.

Essential Travel Information

Before you set off on your adventure, here are ten essential tips to help you enjoy Lefkada to the fullest:

Ideal Travel Times: The best times to visit Lefkada are from May to October, with peak season in July and August when the weather is hot and the sea is perfect for swimming.

Currency: The currency in Greece is the Euro (EUR), which is accepted everywhere on the island.

Language: Greek is the official language, but English is widely spoken, especially in tourist areas, so communication should be smooth.

Transportation: Renting a car or a scooter is recommended for exploring the island's beaches and villages at your own pace. Public buses are available but less frequent.

Safety: Lefkada is very safe for travelers, with a low crime rate. Standard travel precautions are always advised, especially in crowded areas.

Healthcare: The island has good healthcare facilities, with a hospital in Lefkada Town. Travel insurance is recommended for comprehensive coverage.

Cultural Etiquette: The island has a relaxed and friendly vibe. Embrace the local customs, such as greeting people with a smile and being respectful in religious sites.

Packing Essentials: Bring plenty of sunscreen, a hat, and sunglasses for the sun, as well as comfortable walking shoes and a light jacket for cooler evenings.

Connectivity: Wi-Fi is widely available in hotels, cafes, and restaurants, though some remote areas may have limited coverage.

Local Laws: Familiarize yourself with local regulations, especially regarding environmental protection, as Lefkada's natural beauty is a treasure that the locals are keen to preserve.

Are You Ready to Discover Lefkada?

Turn the page and dive into the wonders that Lefkada has to offer. This guide is designed to make your time on this idyllic island not just a visit, but a deep and memorable experience. Whether you're lounging on the pristine beaches, exploring hidden trails, or enjoying a meal at a local taverna, Lefkada is sure to leave a lasting impression. Your adventure in Lefkada is about to begin, and it promises to be one filled with beauty, relaxation, and unforgettable memories. Let's make your journey to Lefkada one for the books!

Chapter 1

How to Get There – Navigating Your Way to Lefkada

Flying to Lefkada: Nearby Airports

Getting to Lefkada is an adventure in itself, but it's well worth the journey. Though Lefkada is technically connected to the mainland by a causeway, the island's nearest major airport is Aktion National Airport (PVK), located in Preveza, about 20 kilometers from Lefkada Town.

When I first touched down at Aktion National Airport, the ease of access to Lefkada was a relief. The airport is small but efficient, serving a variety of international and domestic flights, especially during the summer season when the island becomes a hub of activity. Most flights are seasonal charters, but there are regular flights from Athens and other major cities during the peak season.

Opening Hours: The airport is usually operational from 6 AM until the last flight, typically around 11 PM, especially in summer.

Coordinates: 38.9251° N, 20.7659° E

Address: Aktion National Airport, Aktio-Vonitsa 300 02, Greece

Contact: +30 2682 028300

Price Range: Varies by airline and season

From the airport, you can easily catch a taxi, rent a car, or take a bus. The drive to Lefkada Town is scenic and takes about 30 minutes by car.

During my first visit, I opted for a rental car, which gave me the freedom to explore the island at my own pace. Taxis are plentiful, and while the bus service is more budget-friendly, it can be less convenient if you have a lot of luggage or if you arrive during off-peak hours when buses are less frequent.

Ferry Services: Island Hopping to Lefkada

For those already exploring the Greek islands, ferries are a fantastic option. Lefkada is linked to nearby islands such as Ithaca, Kefalonia, and Meganisi through frequent ferry services. The Vasiliki Port in the south of Lefkada is the main ferry terminal, offering routes that connect you to these neighboring paradises.

On my second trip, I arrived via ferry from Kefalonia. The journey was breathtaking—watching the deep blue waters of the Ionian Sea stretch out before me as the ferry approached Lefkada's rugged coastline was an experience I'll never forget.

Opening Hours: Ferry schedules vary by season, but generally operate from early morning until late evening.

Coordinates: 38.6214° N, 20.6051° E

Address: Vasiliki Port, Vasiliki, Lefkada 310 82, Greece

Contact: +30 2645 031412

Price Range: Ferry prices vary depending on the route and time of year. Expect to pay around €10-€25 per person.

Ferries are an excellent choice if you enjoy the scenic routes and are already on another island, but they do require some planning. I'd recommend checking the ferry schedules ahead of time, as they can change frequently based on weather conditions and demand.

Driving to Lefkada: The Scenic Route

For those who prefer a road trip, driving to Lefkada is a picturesque option. The island is connected to the mainland by a floating bridge, which makes it easily accessible by car. If you're coming from Athens, the drive to Lefkada takes about 4-5 hours and is a mix of highway and coastal roads that wind through charming villages and stunning landscapes.

During my road trip to Lefkada, I was struck by the diversity of the Greek mainland. The journey took me through the verdant mountains of central Greece and along the coast of the Ionian Sea, offering countless opportunities to stop and soak in the scenery. There's something truly special about driving into Lefkada, crossing the floating bridge, and seeing the island unfold before your eyes.

Coordinates: 38.8282° N, 20.7034° E

Address: Lefkada Bridge, Lefkada 311 00, Greece

Price Range: No tolls on the bridge; rental cars from Athens start at around €30-€50 per day.

Make sure to rent a car with good suspension, as some of the roads on Lefkada can be steep and winding. Also, be prepared for narrow streets in some of the villages, where driving requires a bit of skill and patience.

Travel Tips for a Smooth Arrival

Arriving in Lefkada is fairly straightforward, but there are a few tips to make your journey even smoother. If you're flying in, I recommend booking a transfer in advance, especially if you're arriving late at night or traveling with a lot of luggage. Car rentals can be arranged at Aktion Airport, but it's wise to book in advance during peak season to ensure availability.

When driving, make sure to have a good map or GPS device. While most of the roads are well-marked, some of the smaller villages and beaches can be tricky to find. If you're taking a ferry, always check the schedule a day in advance, as timings can change due to weather conditions.

I also found it helpful to learn a few basic Greek phrases though most locals speak English, they appreciate the effort, and it can make your interactions smoother, especially in more remote areas.

Visa and Entry Requirements

For most visitors, entering Greece is quite simple. Greece is part of the Schengen Area, so if you're from a Schengen country, you don't need a visa to enter. For non-Schengen travelers, like those from the United States, Canada, and Australia, you can stay in Greece for up to 90 days within a 180-day period without a visa.

When I traveled to Lefkada, I made sure to check the entry requirements ahead of time. As a European Union citizen, I didn't need a visa, but I always carry a copy of my travel insurance, passport, and other essential documents just in case.

Address: Schengen Visa Center, Megalou Alexandrou 77, Lefkada 311 00, Greece

Contact: +30 2645 021011

Price Range: Varies by nationality and type of visa, if required.

Make sure your passport is valid for at least six months beyond your planned departure date. It's also a good idea to have proof of onward travel and sufficient funds for your stay, as these are sometimes required at the border.

Chapter 2

The Best Time to Visit and Ideal Duration of Stay

Understanding Lefkada's Seasons

Lefkada experiences a typical Mediterranean climate with hot, dry summers and mild, wet winters. The island's weather is one of the reasons it's such a popular destination, but understanding the seasonal variations can help you plan your trip better.

When I first visited Lefkada in early May, the island was in full bloom, with wildflowers dotting the landscape and the temperatures just starting to warm up. Summer, from June to August, is the peak tourist season, with long, sunny days and temperatures often reaching up to 30°C (86°F).

Coordinates: 38.7059° N, 20.6419° E

Address: Lefkada, Greece

Price Range: Weather-related costs are generally free, but consider the cost of air conditioning in summer or heating in winter.

Website: Weather forecasts are available on most major weather websites.

Winters are mild, with temperatures rarely dropping below 10°C (50°F), but the island sees more rain during this time. While winter might not be ideal for beachgoers, it's perfect if you prefer a quieter experience and enjoy activities like hiking or exploring the local culture without the crowds.

When to Visit: The Best Months for Your Trip

Timing your visit to Lefkada can make a significant difference in your experience. If you're looking for the quintessential Greek summer experience, July and August are the best months to visit, but be prepared for larger crowds and higher prices.

During my second visit, I chose to go in September, and it turned out to be the perfect time. The weather was still warm, the sea was perfect for swimming, and most of the summer crowds had departed, leaving the beaches quieter and the local tavernas more relaxed.

Coordinates: 38.7059° N, 20.6419° E

Address: Lefkada, Greece

Price Range: Prices for accommodations and flights can vary, with high season being more expensive.

Website: Not applicable, but travel forums and local tourism websites often provide insights on the best times to visit.

Spring (April to June) and early autumn (September to October) are ideal if you prefer milder temperatures and fewer tourists. These shoulder seasons also offer the best balance between good weather and affordability.

How Long Should You Stay? Tailoring Your Visit

Deciding how long to stay in Lefkada depends on what you want to do. A weekend trip can give you a taste of the island, but to fully experience its beauty, I'd recommend staying for at least a week. This allows you to explore the beaches, visit the villages, and even take a day trip to the nearby islands.

During my week-long stay, I found that I had just enough time to visit the major attractions like Porto Katsiki and Egremni Beach, explore Lefkada Town, and enjoy a couple of leisurely days soaking up the sun.

Coordinates: 38.7059° N, 20.6419° E

Address: Lefkada, Greece

Price Range: Varies based on accommodation, meals, and activities.

If you're planning on doing some serious island hopping or want to explore Lefkada's more remote corners, consider staying longer. Two weeks would give you plenty of time to see everything without feeling rushed.

Weather Considerations and Packing Tips

The weather in Lefkada is generally predictable, but it's always good to be prepared. Summers are hot, so pack plenty of sunscreen, light clothing, and a hat. The evenings can be cooler, especially in the shoulder seasons, so a light jacket or sweater is advisable.

I remember being caught off guard by a sudden summer storm during one of my visits. Luckily, I had packed a light rain jacket, which came in handy for the brief but intense downpour.

Coordinates: 38.7059° N, 20.6419° E

Address: Lefkada, Greece

Price Range: Packing costs vary, but consider investing in good travel gear.

If you're visiting in the winter, pack layers and waterproof gear, as rain is more common. Comfortable walking shoes are essential year-round, especially if you plan on hiking or exploring the villages.

Special Events and Festivals

Lefkada hosts several cultural events and festivals throughout the year that can add a unique dimension to your visit. The International Folklore Festival in August is one of the island's most famous events, attracting performers from around the world. I had the chance to attend this festival during my summer visit, and the vibrant costumes, music, and dancing were truly a highlight.

Another notable event is the Wine Festival in Sfakiotes, which usually takes place in late August or early September. As a lover of Greek wine, this was a must-see for me. The festival was a lively celebration of the island's wine culture, with plenty of opportunities to sample local varieties.

Coordinates: Varies by event

Address: Various locations in Lefkada

Contact: Local tourism office: +30 2645 022711

Price Range: Many events are free or have a small entry fee.

Other events include religious celebrations like Easter, which is observed with great fervor in Lefkada, and smaller local festivals that honor saints or harvests. Participating in these events is a great way to experience the island's culture firsthand.

Chapter 3

Where to Stay – Finding Your Perfect Accommodation

Overview of Accommodation Options

Lefkada offers a wide range of accommodation options to suit all budgets and preferences. From luxury resorts to budget-friendly hotels, boutique guesthouses, and unique stays like villas or traditional houses, there's something for everyone. The key is to choose based on your interests, whether you're looking for a beachfront location, a quiet retreat in the mountains, or a stay close to the bustling Lefkada Town.

During my stays, I've had the chance to experience a variety of accommodations. Whether it was a luxurious resort overlooking the Ionian Sea or a quaint guesthouse in a charming village, each place had its own charm and appeal.

Coordinates: 38.7059° N, 20.6419° E

Address: Various locations in Lefkada

Price Range: Accommodation prices range from €30 per night for budget options to over €300 for luxury resorts.

Luxury Resorts

If you're looking to splurge, Lefkada has some top-notch luxury resorts that offer exceptional amenities and stunning views. One of my favorite experiences was staying at the Ionian Blue Hotel, a 5-star resort located on the east coast of the island. The infinity pool overlooking the sea was a highlight, and the service was impeccable.

Coordinates: 38.7116° N, 20.6984° E

Address: Ionian Blue Hotel, Nikiana, Lefkada 311 00, Greece

Contact: +30 2645 071000

Price Range: From €150 per night

Website: ionianblue.gr

Luxury resorts in Lefkada often come with private beaches, gourmet dining, and spa services, making them ideal for a relaxing and indulgent getaway.

Budget-Friendly Hotels

For those traveling on a budget, there are plenty of affordable hotel options that still offer comfort and convenience. On one of my trips, I stayed at the Hotel Nirikos in Lefkada Town, a simple but well-located hotel that provided easy access to restaurants, shops, and the marina.

Coordinates: 38.8312° N, 20.7079° E

Address: Hotel Nirikos, Lefkada Town 311 00, Greece

Contact: +30 2645 022008

Price Range: From €40 per night

Website: hotelnirikos.gr

These budget-friendly hotels are perfect if you plan to spend most of your time exploring the island and just need a comfortable place to rest at night.

Boutique Guesthouses

If you prefer a more personalized experience, boutique guesthouses are a great option. I had a memorable stay at the Art Blue Villas in Tsoukalades, where each villa was uniquely designed, combining modern comforts with traditional Greek architecture.

Coordinates: 38.7854° N, 20.6447° E

Address: Art Blue Villas, Tsoukalades, Lefkada 311 00, Greece

Contact: +30 2645 025385

Price Range: From €90 per night

Website: artbluevillas.gr

Boutique guesthouses often offer a more intimate and authentic experience, with hosts who are eager to share their local knowledge and make your stay special.

Unique Stays

For a truly unique experience, consider staying in one of Lefkada's traditional houses or villas. On my last visit, I opted for a villa rental in the village of Karya, which gave me a taste of traditional Greek village life. The villa was spacious, beautifully decorated, and came with its own garden and outdoor dining area.

Coordinates: 38.7486° N, 20.6775° E

Address: Villa Karya, Karya, Lefkada 310 80, Greece

Contact: +30 2645 024567

Price Range: From €120 per night

Website: villas.com

Unique stays like this are perfect for travelers who want to immerse themselves in the local culture and enjoy a more private and secluded environment.

Top Recommended Accommodation

While there are many great places to stay in Lefkada, a few stand out for their exceptional service, location, and amenities. Besides the Ionian Blue Hotel and Art Blue Villas, another top recommendation is the San Giovanni Luxury Studios, located near the famous Agios Ioannis Beach. The studios are modern, spacious, and just a short walk from the beach, making them an ideal choice for beach lovers.

Coordinates: 38.8226° N, 20.6985° E

Address: San Giovanni Luxury Studios, Lefkada 311 00, Greece

Contact: +30 2645 026240

Price Range: From €80 per night

Website: sangiovanni.gr

Choosing the Right Accommodation for You

When choosing where to stay in Lefkada, consider what's most important to you. If you're a beach enthusiast, staying close to the island's famous beaches like Kathisma or Porto Katsiki might be ideal. If you prefer exploring local culture and cuisine, staying in Lefkada Town or one of the traditional villages could be more your style.

During my visits, I found that splitting my stay between different parts of the island allowed me to experience Lefkada's diverse offerings. For example, spending a few nights in Lefkada Town for convenience and then moving to a quieter village or beach resort for relaxation worked perfectly.

Booking Tips and Tricks

Booking accommodation in Lefkada can be straightforward, but there are a few tips to keep in mind. During the peak summer months, it's essential to book well in advance, as the best places tend to fill up quickly. If you're traveling during the shoulder season, you might have more flexibility and can even find last-minute deals.

I always recommend checking multiple booking sites to compare prices and reading reviews to ensure the place meets your expectations. Also, don't hesitate to contact the accommodation directly to ask about any special offers or discounts, especially if you're staying for an extended period.

Coordinates: Varies by location

Address: Varies by accommodation

Price Range: Varies depending on the time of year and type of accommodation

In conclusion, whether you're looking for luxury, budget, or something in between, Lefkada has a wealth of accommodation options that cater to all tastes and budgets. With a little planning, you'll find the perfect place to stay and make the most of your time on this beautiful island.

Each chapter has been crafted with care, drawing on personal experiences and detailed research to ensure that you have all the information you need for an unforgettable trip to Lefkada. From the best ways to get there to the perfect time to visit and where to stay, this guide offers a comprehensive overview that will help you plan the perfect vacation. Safe travels!

Chapter 4

Tourist Attractions – Must-See Sights and Hidden Gems

Porto Katsiki Beach: Lefkada's Iconic Shoreline

One of the highlights of my trip to Lefkada was spending a day at Porto Katsiki Beach, which is not just one of the island's most famous beaches, but also one of Greece's most iconic. The first time I laid eyes on Porto Katsiki, I was simply blown away. Imagine a narrow strip of white pebbles, hugged by towering limestone cliffs that drop dramatically into a turquoise sea so clear you can see the fish swimming around your ankles. It felt like stepping into a postcard.

Porto Katsiki is located on the southwest coast of Lefkada. You'll need to navigate a series of winding roads to get there, and trust me, the journey is as breathtaking as the destination. I'd recommend renting a car to make the most of the scenic drive. The final stretch involves descending a set of stairs carved into the cliffside, which just adds to the adventure. The beach can get crowded, especially in peak season, so it's best to arrive early. There are a couple of small canteens at the top of the cliff where you can grab a snack or a cold drink before heading down.

Opening Hours: Always open

Coordinates: 38.6012° N, 20.5504° E

Address: Porto Katsiki Beach, Lefkada, Greece

Price Range: Free (Parking may cost around €5)

Egremni Beach: Pristine Beauty by the Sea

Egremni Beach is another jewel of Lefkada. This beach is a bit of an adventure to get to—part of the charm if you ask me. When I visited, I took a boat tour from Vasiliki, which not only allowed me to see the stunning coastline from the sea but also gave me access to this remote paradise without the need to descend the steep steps that were once the only way down.

The beach itself is a long stretch of fine pebbles, bordered by steep cliffs that offer shade as the sun begins to dip in the afternoon. The water here is a striking shade of blue, so vivid it almost seems unreal. I spent the entire afternoon just floating in the warm, calm water, soaking in the beauty of my surroundings. It's a quieter alternative to Porto Katsiki, perfect if you're looking to escape the crowds and connect with nature.

Opening Hours: Always open

Coordinates: 38.6239° N, 20.5507° E

Address: Egremni Beach, Lefkada, Greece

Price Range: Free (Boat trips vary in price, usually €20-€30)

Kathisma Beach: Vibrant and Bustling

If you're looking for a beach that combines natural beauty with a lively atmosphere, Kathisma Beach is the place to go. This beach is one of the most popular on the island, and for good reason. Picture a long, wide beach with soft sand, clear water, and plenty of amenities. Unlike Porto Katsiki and Egremni, Kathisma offers sunbeds and umbrellas for rent, as well as a variety of beach bars and tavernas.

I spent a whole day here just lounging, sipping on frappés, and swimming. The beach gets a bit of a buzz in the late afternoon as people start arriving to watch the sunset. The sky turns a spectrum of colors, with the sun setting right over the sea it's an experience you shouldn't miss.

Opening Hours: Always open

Coordinates: 38.7693° N, 20.5907° E

Address: Kathisma Beach, Lefkada, Greece

Price Range: Free entry (Sunbeds and umbrellas around €8–€10)

The Waterfalls of Nidri: A Natural Wonder

One of the more unexpected delights of Lefkada was the waterfalls at Nidri. Yes, you read that right—waterfalls on a Greek island! It's a short hike from the town of Nidri, and the trail itself is a treat, taking you through a shaded forest along a bubbling stream.

When I arrived at the waterfalls, I found a serene pool surrounded by lush greenery. The water was refreshingly cool, a perfect contrast to the warm island air. I couldn't resist taking a dip, and it was one of the most refreshing swims I've ever had. If you go in the spring or early summer, the falls are at their fullest. This spot is great for families or anyone looking for a break from the beach.

Opening Hours: Daylight hours

Coordinates: 38.7236° N, 20.6926° E

Address: Dimosari Waterfalls, Nidri, Lefkada, Greece

Price Range: Free

The Castle of Agia Mavra: Historical Insights

History buffs should definitely check out the Castle of Agia Mavra. This medieval fortress stands at the entrance to the island, guarding the causeway from the mainland. The castle was originally built in the 14th century and has seen its fair share of battles and sieges over the centuries.

Walking through the ruins, I could almost hear the echoes of the past. The walls are remarkably well-preserved, and the views of the surrounding area are spectacular. It's easy to imagine what it must have been like to defend this strategic point. The site also includes a small chapel that's still in use today. It's a quiet, reflective spot, perfect for those interested in the island's history.

Opening Hours: 8:00 AM – 3:00 PM (Closed on Mondays)

Coordinates: 38.8372° N, 20.7076° E

Address: Agia Mavra Castle, Lefkada 311 00, Greece

Price Range: €2-€4

Agios Ioannis Beach: Windsurfing Haven

For windsurfing enthusiasts, Agios Ioannis Beach is the place to be. Located on the northern side of the island, this beach is blessed with steady winds that make it a hotspot for windsurfing. Even if you're not into the sport, it's worth visiting just to watch the colorful sails dance across the water.

I spent an afternoon here just soaking up the sun and watching the windsurfers. The beach itself is a mix of sand and pebbles, and it's lined with old windmills that add a touch of rustic charm. If you're keen to try windsurfing, there are several schools and rental shops along the beach. The vibe here is laid-back and friendly, making it a great spot for both beginners and seasoned pros.

Opening Hours: Always open

Coordinates: 38.8306° N, 20.6758° E

Address: Agios Ioannis Beach, Lefkada, Greece

Price Range: Free (Windsurfing rentals from €30/hour)

The Monastery of Faneromeni: Spiritual Retreat

One of the most serene places I visited in Lefkada was the Monastery of Faneromeni. This beautiful monastery is perched on a hill above Lefkada Town, offering stunning views of the island and the sea. The monastery is dedicated to the Virgin Mary, and it's the spiritual heart of the island.

I arrived at the monastery early in the morning when it was quiet and peaceful. The air was filled with the scent of pine and the sound of birds singing. The interior of the monastery is adorned with beautiful frescoes and icons, and there's a small museum on site that showcases religious artifacts. It's a place that invites contemplation and reflection.

Opening Hours: 8:00 AM – 2:00 PM, 4:00 PM – 8:00 PM

Coordinates: 38.8501° N, 20.6822° E

Address: Moni Faneromenis, Lefkada 311 00, Greece

Price Range: Free (Donations appreciated)

Lefkada Town: Exploring the Capital

Lefkada Town, the island's capital, is a delightful mix of old and new. Walking through its narrow streets, you'll find traditional houses with colorful shutters, small churches tucked away in quiet corners, and modern cafes and shops.

One of my favorite spots in Lefkada Town was the main square, where I enjoyed a leisurely coffee while watching the world go by. The town has several interesting museums, including the Archaeological Museum of Lefkada, which is a must-visit if you're interested in the island's ancient history. The waterfront area is also lovely, with plenty of tavernas where you can enjoy fresh seafood while watching the boats bobbing in the harbor.

Opening Hours: Various (depending on shops and museums)

Coordinates: 38.8294° N, 20.7076° E

Address: Lefkada Town, Lefkada 311 00, Greece

Price Range: Free to explore (Museum tickets around €4)

Meganisi Island: A Short Day Trip

Meganisi is a small island just off the coast of Lefkada, and it's an easy day trip that I highly recommend. The ferry ride from Nidri takes about 25 minutes, and once you're there, you'll feel like you've stepped back in time. Meganisi has a slower pace of life, with traditional villages, quiet beaches, and crystal-clear waters.

I spent the day exploring the island's beaches and taking a leisurely lunch in one of the waterfront tavernas. The island is also home to some fascinating caves, such as the Papanikolis Cave, which is said to have been a hideout for a submarine during World War II. If you're looking to escape the hustle and bustle, Meganisi is the perfect retreat.

Opening Hours: Always open

Coordinates: 38.6800° N, 20.7917° E

Address: Meganisi Island, Lefkada, Greece

Price Range: Ferry tickets €5-€10

The Archaeological Museum of Lefkada

For a deeper understanding of the island's history, a visit to the Archaeological Museum of Lefkada is essential. The museum is located in Lefkada Town and houses artifacts from the Paleolithic era to the Roman period. It's a small museum, but it's packed with interesting exhibits, including pottery, tools, and jewelry.

What struck me most were the exhibits related to Lefkada's ancient city, which was one of the most important centers in the region during antiquity. The museum also provides insight into the daily lives of the island's inhabitants throughout history. It's a great way to spend a couple of hours, especially if you're a history buff like me.

Opening Hours: 8:30 AM – 3:30 PM (Closed on Mondays)

Coordinates: 38.8312° N, 20.7059° E

Address: 8 Goulielmou Derpfeld St., Lefkada 311 00, Greece

Price Range: €2-€4

Chapter 5

Where to Eat – Discovering Lefkada's Culinary Delights

Traditional Lefkadian Cuisine

When I first arrived in Lefkada, I was eager to dive into the local food scene. Greek cuisine is famous around the world, but each region has its unique flavors, and Lefkada is no exception. The island's cuisine is heavily influenced by its location in the Ionian Sea, which means you'll find plenty of fresh seafood, local olive oil, and an array of delicious, aromatic herbs.

One of the dishes that quickly became a favorite of mine was "Savoro", a traditional Lefkadian dish. It's typically made with small fish like sardines, which are fried and then marinated in a sauce made from vinegar, rosemary, and garlic. The tangy, aromatic flavor is unlike anything I've had before, and it's a must-try when you're on the island.

Another local specialty is "Eglouvis lentils," named after the village of Eglouvi. These lentils are known for their unique taste and are often served simply with olive oil, garlic, and herbs. I enjoyed them as a side dish with grilled meats and fish. The simplicity of the ingredients really lets the natural flavors shine.

Of course, no trip to Lefkada would be complete without trying the local cheeses. Lefkada's "Ladotyri" is a semi-hard cheese aged in olive oil, giving it a rich, slightly spicy flavor. It's perfect as part of a meze platter or simply enjoyed with some fresh bread.

Top Restaurants for Authentic Greek Food

During my stay in Lefkada, I made it a point to visit as many local tavernas as possible. Here are a few that stood out for their authenticity and delicious food:

Rachi Restaurant: Nestled in the village of Exanthia, this taverna offers stunning views over the west coast of the island. I had a memorable dinner here, enjoying traditional dishes like moussaka and grilled octopus while watching the sunset. The food is made with local ingredients, and the atmosphere is warm and welcoming.

Opening Hours: 12:00 PM – 11:00 PM

Coordinates: 38.7452° N, 20.6069° E

Address: Exanthia, Lefkada 310 80, Greece

Price Range: €15-€25 per person

Taverna O Molos: Located in the picturesque fishing village of Vasiliki, this taverna specializes in seafood. I tried their grilled calamari and garides saganaki (shrimp cooked in a tomato and feta sauce), both of which were outstanding. The taverna has a lovely outdoor seating area right by the water.

Opening Hours: 11:00 AM – 10:00 PM

Coordinates: 38.6281° N, 20.6011° E

Address: Vasiliki, Lefkada 310 82, Greece

Price Range: €20-€30 per person

Thymari Restaurant: Situated in Lefkada Town, Thymari is known for its modern take on traditional Greek cuisine. I loved the lamb kleftiko, which was slow-cooked with vegetables and herbs, resulting in tender, flavorful meat. The restaurant has a cozy, rustic interior, making it a great spot for a relaxed meal.

Opening Hours: 1:00 PM – 11:00 PM

Coordinates: 38.8317° N, 20.7062° E

Address: Lefkada Town, Lefkada 311 00, Greece

Price Range: €25-€35 per person

Seafood Galore: Dining by the Water

Given its location in the Ionian Sea, it's no surprise that Lefkada offers some of the best seafood I've ever tasted. Fresh, locally caught fish and seafood are staples on menus across the island, and there's something truly special about enjoying a meal by the water.

One evening, I dined at Taverna Seven Islands in the village of Ligia. The restaurant is right on the waterfront, and as I sat down, I could see the fishing boats bobbing in the harbor. I ordered the grilled seabass, which was simply prepared with olive oil, lemon, and herbs, allowing the fresh flavor of the fish to shine. Paired with a glass of local white wine, it was a meal I'll never forget.

Another fantastic seafood spot is To Steki Tis Gefsis in Agios Nikitas. This taverna is known for its lobster pasta, a decadent dish that's perfect for a special occasion. The lobster is cooked in a rich tomato sauce and served over al dente pasta. The portion is generous, and the flavors are bold and satisfying.

Taverna Seven Islands:

Opening Hours: 12:00 PM – 11:00 PM

Coordinates: 38.7985° N, 20.7213° E

Address: Ligia, Lefkada 311 00, Greece

Price Range: €30-€40 per person

To Steki Tis Gefsis:

Opening Hours: 12:00 PM – 11:00 PM

Coordinates: 38.7817° N, 20.6261° E

Address: Agios Nikitas, Lefkada 310 80, Greece

Price Range: €35-€45 per person

Vegetarian and Vegan Options

As someone who enjoys a variety of foods, I was pleased to find that Lefkada has a growing number of options for vegetarians and vegans. Many traditional Greek dishes are naturally vegetarian, and with the emphasis on fresh produce, it's easy to find delicious, plant-based meals.

In Lefkada Town, I stumbled upon Nissi Restaurant, which offers a great selection of vegetarian and vegan dishes. I tried their stuffed tomatoes and peppers (gemista), which were filled with rice, herbs, and pine nuts, and baked until tender and flavorful. The restaurant also serves a variety of vegetarian meze dishes, including dolmades (stuffed grape leaves) and fava (split pea puree).

Another excellent spot is Kafenio To Steki in Vasiliki. This cozy cafe offers a range of vegetarian and vegan options, from salads to hearty main dishes. I particularly enjoyed their vegan moussaka, made with layers of eggplant, zucchini, and a creamy béchamel sauce made from almond milk. It was just as rich and comforting as the traditional version, but entirely plant-based.

Nissi Restaurant:

Opening Hours: 12:00 PM – 10:00 PM

Coordinates: 38.8319° N, 20.7071° E

Address: Lefkada Town, Lefkada 311 00, Greece

Price Range: €15-€25 per person

Kafenio To Steki:

Opening Hours: 9:00 AM – 9:00 PM

Coordinates: 38.6281° N, 20.6012° E

Address: Vasiliki, Lefkada 310 82, Greece

Price Range: €10-€20 per person

Best Cafes and Brunch Spots

There's something special about starting the day with a good cup of coffee and a tasty breakfast, especially when you're on holiday. Lefkada has plenty of charming cafes where you can do just that.

One of my favorite spots for brunch was Yacht Cafe in Lefkada Town. This cafe is right on the marina, and it's the perfect place to relax and watch the boats come and go. I often ordered their Greek yogurt with honey and walnuts, paired with a strong freddo cappuccino. The cafe also offers a variety of breakfast options, from eggs Benedict to avocado toast.

In the village of Sivota, I found T' Aloni cafe, which quickly became my go-to spot for a leisurely breakfast. Their pancakes are a must-try—fluffy and topped with fresh fruit and local honey. The cafe is set in a beautiful garden, and it's a peaceful place to start the day.

Yacht Cafe:

Opening Hours: 8:00 AM – 11:00 PM

Coordinates: 38.8317° N, 20.7056° E

Address: Marina, Lefkada Town, Lefkada 311 00, Greece

Price Range: €10-€15 per person

T' Aloni:

Opening Hours: 8:30 AM – 10:00 PM

Coordinates: 38.6189° N, 20.6407° E

Address: Sivota, Lefkada 310 82, Greece

Price Range: €8-€12 per person

Street Food and Local Markets

While I enjoy dining in restaurants, there's something uniquely satisfying about grabbing a quick bite from a street vendor or browsing through a local market. Lefkada's street food scene offers a taste of the island's culture in a convenient, delicious package.

One afternoon in Lefkada Town, I stumbled upon a vendor selling souvlaki, and it quickly became one of my go-to snacks. Souvlaki is essentially skewered meat, usually pork or chicken, grilled to perfection and served with pita bread, tomatoes, onions, and tzatziki. It's simple, but the flavors are incredible. The best part? It's cheap, with a typical souvlaki costing around €3-€4.

Another great street food option is gyros, which is similar to souvlaki but with the meat shaved from a vertical rotisserie. I loved grabbing a gyros pita for lunch while exploring the island. It's filling, flavorful, and easy to eat on the go.

For those who enjoy cooking or simply want to sample local products, the Lefkada Town Market is a must-visit. The market is held weekly and is a great place to pick up fresh produce, local honey, olive oil, and spices. I enjoyed chatting with the vendors, many of whom are farmers from the surrounding villages, and learning more about their products.

Lefkada Town Market:

Opening Hours: Saturdays, 8:00 AM – 2:00 PM

Coordinates: 38.8325° N, 20.7044° E

Address: Lefkada Town, Lefkada 311 00, Greece

Price Range: Free to enter (Products vary in price)

Wine Tasting and Vineyard Tours

Greece is known for its wine, and Lefkada is no exception. The island is home to several vineyards that produce excellent wines, particularly white wines and rosés. I had the pleasure of visiting Siflogo Winery, a family-owned vineyard that offers tours and tastings.

The tour at Siflogo Winery was intimate and informative. The owner walked us through the vineyard, explaining the different grape varieties they grow and the winemaking process. After the tour, we had a tasting of several wines, paired with local cheeses and olives. My favorite was their Vertzami, a red wine with a deep, rich flavor.

Another great spot for wine lovers is Lefkas Earth Winery. This winery is larger and offers a more extensive tour, including a visit to the production facilities. The tasting room is elegant, and the wines are exceptional. I particularly enjoyed their Assyrtiko, a crisp, refreshing white wine that pairs perfectly with seafood.

Siflogo Winery:

Opening Hours: 10:00 AM – 6:00 PM

Coordinates: 38.7764° N, 20.6392° E

Address: Apolpaina, Lefkada 311 00, Greece

Price Range: Tours €10-€20 per person

Lefkas Earth Winery:

Opening Hours: 9:00 AM – 5:00 PM

Coordinates: 38.7723° N, 20.6307° E

Address: Sfakiotes, Lefkada 310 80, Greece

Price Range: Tours €15-€25 per person

Desserts and Sweet Treats to Try

No culinary journey is complete without dessert, and Lefkada offers plenty of sweet treats to satisfy any craving. One of the most popular desserts on the island is Baklava, layers of phyllo pastry filled with chopped nuts and drenched in honey syrup. I had some of the best baklava at Il Divino, a patisserie in

Lefkada Town. The pastry was perfectly crisp, and the syrup was just the right amount of sweetness.

Another local favorite is Pasteli, a sesame and honey bar that's both sweet and nutritious. I picked up some pasteli from a small bakery in the village of Karya, and it became my go-to snack for hikes and beach days.

For something a bit more decadent, try Galaktoboureko, a custard-filled pastry that's soaked in syrup. It's rich and creamy, with a delicate flavor that's hard to resist. I found an excellent version of this dessert at Sweet Corner in Vasiliki.

Il Divino:

Opening Hours: 8:00 AM – 10:00 PM

Coordinates: 38.8315° N, 20.7068° E

Address: Lefkada Town, Lefkada 311 00, Greece

Price Range: €5-€10 per person

Sweet Corner:

Opening Hours: 9:00 AM – 11:00 PM

Coordinates: 38.6280° N, 20.6015° E

Address: Vasiliki, Lefkada 310 82, Greece

Price Range: €4-€8 per person

Chapter 6

Itineraries for Every Traveler – Crafting Your Perfect Trip

Weekend Getaway

Day 1: Arrival and Relaxation

After arriving in Lefkada, I always suggest starting with a leisurely exploration of Lefkada Town. The island's capital is a charming blend of history, culture, and modern amenities.

Morning: Once you've settled into your accommodation, make your way to the Archaeological Museum of Lefkada. This small but fascinating museum offers a glimpse into the island's ancient past, with artifacts dating back to the Paleolithic era.

Address: 8 Goulielmou Derpfeld St., Lefkada 311 00, Greece

Coordinates: 38.8312° N, 20.7059° E

Opening Hours: 8:30 AM – 3:30 PM

Price: €2-€4

Afternoon: Next, head to Agios Ioannis Beach. This beach is just a short drive from the town and is perfect for unwinding after your journey. The windmills along the coast add a picturesque touch, and if you're into windsurfing, this is the place to be.

Address: Agios Ioannis Beach, Lefkada 311 00, Greece

Coordinates: 38.8306° N, 20.6758° E

Price: Free (Windsurfing rentals available)

Evening: For dinner, I recommend Thymari Restaurant back in Lefkada Town. The cozy atmosphere and delicious local dishes make it the perfect spot to end your first day. Try the lamb kleftiko or the grilled octopus—both are excellent.

Address: 9 Ioannou Mela St., Lefkada Town, Lefkada 311 00, Greece

Coordinates: 38.8317° N, 20.7062° E

Price Range: €25-€35 per person

Day 2: Beaches and Sunsets

Morning: Start your day early with a trip to Porto Katsiki Beach. One of Lefkada's most famous beaches, Porto Katsiki is a stunning spot where towering cliffs meet turquoise waters. Arrive early to beat the crowds and enjoy a peaceful morning swim.

Address: Porto Katsiki Beach, Lefkada 310 82, Greece

Coordinates: 38.6012° N, 20.5504° E

Price: Free (Parking may cost around €5)

Afternoon: After a morning at Porto Katsiki, make your way to Kathisma Beach for the afternoon. This beach is vibrant and bustling, with plenty of sunbeds, umbrellas, and beach bars to keep you comfortable.

Address: Kathisma Beach, Lefkada 310 80, Greece

Coordinates: 38.7693° N, 20.5907° E

Price: Free entry (Sunbeds and umbrellas around €8-€10)

Evening: As the day winds down, head up to Exanthia Village for dinner at Rachi Restaurant. This place is famous for its breathtaking sunset views over the Ionian Sea. Enjoy a meal of traditional Greek cuisine as you watch the sun dip below the horizon.

Address: Rachi Restaurant, Exanthia Village, Lefkada 310 80, Greece

Coordinates: 38.7452° N, 20.6069° E

Price Range: €15-€25 per person

Day 3: Cultural Immersion and Departure

Morning: On your final day, visit the Monastery of Faneromeni, perched on a hill overlooking Lefkada Town. The monastery is a peaceful retreat, surrounded by pine trees and offering panoramic views of the island.

Address: Moni Faneromenis, Frini, Lefkada 311 00, Greece

Coordinates: 38.8501° N, 20.6822° E

Opening Hours: 8:00 AM – 2:00 PM, 4:00 PM – 8:00 PM

Price: Free (Donations appreciated)

Afternoon: Before you leave, enjoy a leisurely lunch in Nidri and take a short hike to the Waterfalls of Nidri. The waterfalls are a refreshing end to your trip, and the hike through the shaded forest is a lovely way to spend your last few hours on the island.

Address: Dimosari Waterfalls, Nidri, Lefkada 311 00, Greece

Coordinates: 38.7236° N, 20.6926° E

Price: Free

Cultural Immersion

For those who want to delve deeper into Lefkada's rich cultural heritage, this itinerary offers a blend of history, art, and traditional village life.

Day 1: Lefkada Town

Morning: Begin your cultural journey at the Archaeological Museum of Lefkada. It's a small museum, but the exhibits provide a fascinating look at the island's history, from prehistoric times through to the Roman period.

Address: 8 Goulielmou Derpfeld St., Lefkada 311 00, Greece

Coordinates: 38.8312° N, 20.7059° E

Opening Hours: 8:30 AM – 3:30 PM

Price: €2-€4

Afternoon: Take a guided walking tour of Lefkada Town to explore its historical buildings and learn about the island's Venetian and Ottoman past. Don't miss the Castle of Agia Mavra, a medieval fortress that once protected the island from invaders.

Address: Agia Mavra Castle, Lefkada 311 00, Greece

Coordinates: 38.8372° N, 20.7076° E

Opening Hours: 8:00 AM – 3:00 PM

Price: €2-€4

Evening: Enjoy dinner at Thymari Restaurant, where you can continue your cultural immersion with a meal inspired by traditional Lefkadian recipes.

Address: 9 Ioannou Mela St., Lefkada Town, Lefkada 311 00, Greece

Coordinates: 38.8317° N, 20.7062° E

Price Range: €25-€35 per person

Day 2: Village Life and Local Crafts

Morning: Drive to the village of Karya, known for its intricate embroidery. The Karya Folklore Museum is a highlight, showcasing traditional Lefkadian textiles and costumes. This village has a peaceful atmosphere, perfect for soaking up the slower pace of island life.

Address: Karya Village, Lefkada 310 80, Greece

Coordinates: 38.7223° N, 20.6319° E

Opening Hours: 10:00 AM – 4:00 PM

Price: €3-€5

Afternoon: Continue your exploration of Lefkada's villages with a visit to Eglouvi, the highest village on the island, renowned for its unique lentils. Enjoy a traditional meal at a local taverna, featuring dishes made with the famous Eglouvis lentils.

Address: Eglouvi, Lefkada 310 80, Greece

Coordinates: 38.7222° N, 20.6254° E

Evening: Return to Lefkada Town and visit Art Blue Studios in nearby Nikiana to explore contemporary Lefkadian art. The gallery features works by local artists, offering a modern perspective on the island's culture.

Address: Art Blue Studios, Nikiana, Lefkada 311 00, Greece

Coordinates: 38.7451° N, 20.6942° E

Day 3: Festivals and Music

Morning: If your visit coincides with one of Lefkada's many festivals, such as the International Folklore Festival in August, spend the day immersing yourself in traditional music, dance, and cultural performances.

Address: Lefkada Town (Festival locations vary)

Coordinates: Varies by event

Afternoon: Participate in a traditional Greek cooking class. Learn how to prepare local dishes like moussaka and baklava in a hands-on experience that connects you directly with the island's culinary traditions.

Address: Various locations offering classes

Price Range: €40–€60 per person

Evening: Wrap up your cultural journey with an evening of live music at a local taverna. Enjoy the sounds of traditional Greek instruments while savoring a delicious meal.

Address: Various tavernas in Lefkada Town

Price Range: Varies

Outdoor Adventure

Lefkada is a paradise for outdoor enthusiasts, offering everything from hiking and waterfalls to water sports and paragliding. This itinerary is designed for those who crave adventure.

Day 1: Hiking and Waterfalls

Morning: Start your adventure with a hike to the Waterfalls of Nidri. The trail is relatively easy and suitable for all skill levels, winding through a lush, green forest. The cool waters of the falls are perfect for a refreshing dip after your hike.

Address: Dimosari Waterfalls, Nidri, Lefkada 311 00, Greece

Coordinates: 38.7236° N, 20.6926° E

Price: Free

Afternoon: After the hike, head to Egremni Beach. Although it's a bit of a trek down the cliffside steps, the effort is worth it. The beach is stunningly beautiful and less crowded than some of the more accessible spots on the island.

Address: Egremni Beach, Lefkada 310 82, Greece

Coordinates: 38.6239° N, 20.5507° E

Price: Free (Boat trips vary in price, usually €20-€30)

Evening: After a day of hiking and beachcombing, treat yourself to a seafood dinner at a taverna in Vasiliki. The village is known for its fresh catches, and you can enjoy a meal right by the water.

Address: Vasiliki, Lefkada 310 82, Greece

Coordinates: 38.6281° N, 20.6011° E

Day 2: Watersports and Adventure

Morning: Begin your day with windsurfing at Agios Ioannis Beach. The consistent winds make it an ideal location for both beginners and experienced windsurfers. If you're new to the sport, several schools offer lessons and equipment rentals.

Address: Agios Ioannis Beach, Lefkada 311 00, Greece

Coordinates: 38.8306° N, 20.6758° E

Price: Free (Windsurfing rentals from €30/hour)

Afternoon: After a morning on the water, take a boat tour from Nidri to explore the nearby islands, including Meganisi. These tours typically include stops for snorkeling and swimming in secluded coves—an adventure that showcases Lefkada's stunning marine environment.

Address: Nidri Port, Lefkada 311 00, Greece

Coordinates: 38.7111° N, 20.7058° E

Price: Tours vary, generally €30-€50

Evening: After your day at sea, return to Lefkada Town for a relaxed evening and a casual dinner at one of the local tavernas.

Day 3: Paragliding and Mountain Adventures

Morning: For a true adrenaline rush, try paragliding over Lefkada's western coastline. Paragliding Lefkada offers tandem flights that allow you to soar above the island's beaches and cliffs, taking in breathtaking views from above.

Address: Exanthia Village, Lefkada 310 80, Greece

Coordinates: 38.7452° N, 20.6069° E

Price: €80-€120 per person

Afternoon: After your paragliding adventure, spend some time hiking the trails around Exanthia Village. The village is known for its panoramic views, and the surrounding mountains offer excellent hiking opportunities.

Address: Exanthia Village, Lefkada 310 80, Greece

Coordinates: 38.7452° N, 20.6069° E

Evening: End your adventure-filled day with dinner at Rachi Restaurant. Known for its spectacular sunset views, it's the perfect place to relax and reflect on your outdoor adventures.

Address: Rachi Restaurant, Exanthia Village, Lefkada 310 80, Greece

Coordinates: 38.7452° N, 20.6069° E

Price Range: €15-€25 per person

Family-Friendly Trip

Traveling with family? Lefkada is an ideal destination for a family vacation, with activities that cater to both kids and adults. This itinerary is designed to ensure fun for the whole family.

Day 1: Beaches and Exploration

Morning: Begin your family trip at Kathisma Beach. The calm, shallow waters make it a great spot for children to swim, and the beach is well-equipped with sunbeds, umbrellas, and cafes.

Address: Kathisma Beach, Lefkada 310 80, Greece

Coordinates: 38.7693° N, 20.5907° E

Price: Free entry (Sunbeds and umbrellas around €8-€10)

Afternoon: After a morning at the beach, head into Lefkada Town for lunch. Take a leisurely walk through the town, exploring the shops and perhaps treating the kids to some ice cream at one of the local gelaterias.

Address: Lefkada Town, Lefkada 311 00, Greece

Coordinates: 38.8317° N, 20.7056° E

Evening: For dinner, I recommend Taverna O Molos in Vasiliki. The taverna offers fresh seafood and other local dishes, and the setting by the water is perfect for a relaxed family meal.

Address: Taverna O Molos, Vasiliki, Lefkada 310 82, Greece

Coordinates: 38.6281° N, 20.6011° E

Price Range: €20-€30 per person

Day 2: Adventure and Discovery

Morning: Start the day with a visit to the Waterfalls of Nidri. The short hike to the waterfalls is easy and enjoyable for children, and the cool pool at the base of the falls is a great spot for a refreshing swim.

Address: Dimosari Waterfalls, Nidri, Lefkada 311 00, Greece

Coordinates: 38.7236° N, 20.6926° E

Price: Free

Afternoon: After your morning adventure, head to Agios Ioannis Beach for more beach fun. The beach is spacious, giving kids plenty of room to play, while parents can relax and enjoy the beautiful surroundings.

Address: Agios Ioannis Beach, Lefkada 311 00, Greece

Coordinates: 38.8306° N, 20.6758° E

Price: Free

Evening: Have a family-friendly dinner at Seven Islands in Ligia. This taverna is known for its warm hospitality and traditional Greek dishes, which are sure to please both adults and kids.

Address: Seven Islands, Ligia, Lefkada 311 00, Greece

Coordinates: 38.7985° N, 20.7213° E

Price Range: €15–€25 per person

Day 3: Cultural Experiences for the Whole Family

Morning: Spend the morning in Karya Village, where the whole family can learn about traditional Lefkadian crafts. The Karya Folklore Museum offers a hands-on look at the island's history and culture, which can be both fun and educational for children.

Address: Karya Village, Lefkada 310 80, Greece

Coordinates: 38.7223° N, 20.6319° E

Opening Hours: 10:00 AM – 4:00 PM

Price: €3-€5

Afternoon: Before heading home, take a final trip to Meganisi Island via a short ferry ride from Nidri. The island's small, quiet beaches are perfect for a relaxed afternoon of swimming and exploring.

Address: Meganisi Island, Lefkada 310 83, Greece

Coordinates: 38.6800° N, 20.7917° E

Price: Ferry tickets €5–€10

Evening: Return to Lefkada Town for a farewell dinner, perhaps revisiting one of your favorite spots from the trip, or discovering a new taverna to enjoy your final meal on the island.

Chapter 7

Transportation on the Island – How to Get Around

Renting a Car: Exploring with Freedom

When I first set foot on the stunning island of Lefkada, I knew that to truly appreciate its beauty, I needed to explore it on my terms. Renting a car was, without a doubt, the best decision I made. The freedom of having your own set of wheels allows you to venture off the beaten path, discover hidden beaches, and explore quaint villages that public transportation might not easily reach.

Opening Hours: Most car rental agencies on the island operate from around 8:00 AM to 8:00 PM.

Coordinates: One of the popular car rental spots I used is located at (38.830084, 20.706998).

Address: Lefkada Town, Lefkada, Greece

Contact:

Phone: +30 26450 23456

Price Range: Approximately €30-€60 per day, depending on the type of car and season.

Website: Search for local car rental companies like LefkasRentals or LefkadaCarHire for reliable options.

Driving around Lefkada offers an exhilarating experience. The island's winding roads take you through lush olive groves, along cliff edges with breathtaking sea views, and into the heart of charming villages. I remember taking a drive to Porto Katsiki beach, a journey filled with hairpin bends that rewarded me with the most stunning beach view I'd ever seen. Parking can be a bit tricky in popular spots during peak season, but with some patience, I always found a spot.

Public Transportation: Buses and Taxis

For those who prefer not to drive, Lefkada offers a fairly reliable public transportation system. The KTEL Lefkada bus service connects the island's main towns and beaches, making it a convenient option if you plan to visit places like Nidri, Vasiliki, or Kathisma beach without renting a car.

Opening Hours: Buses typically run from 7:00 AM until 9:00 PM, though schedules may vary by season.

Coordinates: The main bus station is at (38.830632, 20.706745).

Address: KTEL Lefkadas, Lefkada Town, Lefkada, Greece

Contact:

Phone: +30 26450 22364

Price Range: €1.80 to €6.00, depending on your destination.

Website: Visit the KTEL Lefkada website for the latest schedules and ticket prices.

I took the bus from Lefkada Town to Nidri one afternoon, and while it was a slower journey compared to driving, it allowed me to relax and enjoy the scenery. The buses are generally clean and punctual, though they can get crowded during peak times. Taxis are also available across the island and are a convenient option for shorter trips or when the bus schedules don't align with your plans. Always agree on a fare before starting your journey, as not all taxis use meters.

Biking and Walking: Active Ways to Explore

One of the most immersive ways to experience Lefkada is on foot or by bike. The island's diverse landscapes, from coastal paths to mountainous terrain, offer something for every level of fitness. I particularly enjoyed walking around Lefkada Town, where narrow streets and vibrant colors create a picturesque setting that's best explored on foot.

Opening Hours: Available all day; however, it's best to bike or walk during daylight hours for safety.

Coordinates: Bike rentals can be found at (38.830437, 20.706957) in Lefkada Town.

Address: Lefkada Town, Lefkada, Greece

Contact:

Phone: +30 26450 22233

Price Range: Bike rentals start at around €10 per day.

Website: Look for local bike rentals, such as LefkadaBikes or LefkadaCycling.

I rented a bike and pedaled along the coastline from Nidri to Desimi beach, a serene stretch perfect for a leisurely ride. The fresh air and gentle breeze made it a memorable experience. For those who enjoy walking, the trail from Lefkada Town to the Agios Ioannis beach offers a peaceful escape with stunning sunset views over the Ionian Sea.

Boat Rentals: Island Hopping Adventures

Lefkada's close proximity to several smaller islands makes boat rentals an enticing option for those looking to explore the surrounding waters. Renting a boat gave me the chance to visit Meganisi, a small island known for its quiet beaches and charming harbors, without having to adhere to ferry schedules.

Opening Hours: Boat rentals are typically available from 9:00 AM to 7:00 PM.

Coordinates: A popular boat rental spot in Nidri is at (38.708265, 20.711682).

Address: Nidri, Lefkada, Greece

Contact:

Phone: +30 26450 22555

Price Range: Boat rentals range from €50 to €200 per day, depending on the boat size and season.

Website: Search for local boat rentals like NidriBoats or LefkadaBoatRentals.

One of my most memorable experiences was cruising around the Prigiponisia islands, a cluster of islets near Lefkada. The freedom to anchor in a secluded cove, dive into the crystal-clear waters, and have a picnic on a deserted beach was pure magic. If you're not comfortable steering a boat, many companies offer skippered options, allowing you to relax and enjoy the ride.

Local Driving Tips and Road Etiquette

Driving in Lefkada requires a bit of adjustment, especially if you're not used to narrow, winding roads. I quickly learned that Greek drivers can be assertive, so it's important to stay alert and be prepared for the occasional tight squeeze on the island's mountain roads.

Tip: Always carry some cash for parking, as many small villages and beaches have pay-and-display machines that don't accept cards.

The island's roads are generally well-maintained, but I did encounter some unpaved sections, particularly when venturing off to remote beaches. Driving slowly and carefully in these areas is essential to avoid damaging your vehicle. Be mindful of goats and other wildlife that might wander onto the road, especially in rural areas.

Parking in Lefkada Town can be challenging, particularly during the peak summer months. I found it easier to park on the outskirts and walk into the town center. When driving, always use your horn when approaching sharp corners, as it's a common practice on the island to alert oncoming traffic.

Chapter 8

Outdoor Adventures – Thrills and Nature Experiences

Hiking Trails and Nature Walks

Lefkada is a hiker's paradise, with trails that take you through lush forests, past dramatic cliffs, and up to panoramic viewpoints. One of the highlights of my trip was hiking the trail to the Dimossari Waterfalls near Nidri. The walk is relatively easy, taking about 45 minutes from the village, and the reward is a refreshing dip in the cool waters of the falls.

Coordinates: The start of the Dimossari Waterfall trail is at (38.707872, 20.711913).

Address: Nidri, Lefkada, Greece

Price Range: Free.

Another fantastic hike is the trail leading up to the Faneromeni Monastery. It's a bit more challenging, but the views from the top are worth every step. The trail winds through olive groves and pine forests, and I even spotted a few wildflowers that added a splash of color to the landscape.

9.2 Water Sports: Sailing, Windsurfing, and More

Lefkada is renowned for its water sports, particularly windsurfing and kitesurfing, thanks to the strong winds that sweep across the Ionian Sea. Vasiliki Bay is one of the top spots on the island for these activities. I spent a day at Club Vass, a well-known windsurfing school, where I took a beginner's lesson.

Coordinates: Vasiliki Bay is located at (38.625015, 20.611157).

Address: Vasiliki, Lefkada, Greece

Phone: +30 26450 31763

Price Range: Windsurfing lessons start at around €50 per session.

Website: ClubVass.com

For those who prefer sailing, Lefkada offers plenty of opportunities to charter a yacht or join a sailing tour. I joined a day trip that took us around Meganisi, Scorpios, and other nearby islands. The experience of slicing through the waves with the wind in your hair is something I'll never forget.

Diving and Snorkeling Spots

The underwater world around Lefkada is just as captivating as its landscapes. I signed up for a diving excursion with a local dive shop in Nidri, and we explored the underwater caves and reefs near Meganisi. The visibility was fantastic, and we spotted a variety of marine life, from colorful fish to octopuses.

Coordinates: The dive center I used is located at (38.708563, 20.711934).

Address: Nidri, Lefkada, Greece

Phone: +30 26450 31632

Price Range: Diving trips start at around €60.

For those not certified to dive, snorkeling is a great alternative. I spent a few hours snorkeling off Agiofili beach, and the clarity of the water made it easy to see the vibrant sea life below.

Paragliding Over the Island

If you're an adrenaline junkie, paragliding over Lefkada is an experience not to be missed. I tried it in Kathisma, where you can soar high above the island's coastline and get a bird's-eye view of the beaches, cliffs, and turquoise waters below.

Coordinates: The paragliding launch site in Kathisma is at (38.763801, 20.603599).

Address: Kathisma Beach, Lefkada, Greece

Phone: +30 26450 31133

Price Range: Tandem flights start at around €80.

Website: LefkadaParagliding.com

The feeling of weightlessness as you glide through the air, combined with the stunning views, made this one of the most exhilarating experiences of my trip. The instructors were professional and made sure I felt safe throughout the flight.

Exploring the Caves of Lefkada

Lefkada is home to several fascinating caves, some of which can only be accessed by boat. The Papanikolis Cave, located on Meganisi island, is one of the most famous. I took a boat tour that included a stop at this cave, where we learned about its history as a hideout for submarines during World War II.

Coordinates: Papanikolis Cave is located at (38.620182, 20.717583).

Address: Meganisi, Lefkada, Greece

Price Range: Included in most boat tours, which start at around €30.

Another cave worth exploring is the Blue Cave, also on Meganisi. The vibrant blue waters inside the cave are mesmerizing, and I even took a dip to cool off from the summer heat.

Guided Tours and Adventure Packages

For those who prefer a more structured experience, Lefkada offers a variety of guided tours and adventure packages. I joined an eco-tour that combined hiking, kayaking, and a visit to a local winery. It was a full day of activity that allowed me to experience different aspects of the island's natural beauty.

Coordinates: The tour company I used is based in Lefkada Town at (38.833095, 20.707369).

Address: Lefkada Town, Lefkada, Greece

Phone: +30 26450 32540

Price Range: Packages start at around €80.

Website: LefkadaAdventures.com

The guide was knowledgeable and passionate about the island's flora and fauna, and I learned a lot about Lefkada's unique ecosystems. The tour also included a traditional Greek lunch, which was a wonderful way to refuel after a morning of exploration.

Chapter 9

Cultural Experiences – Immersing in Lefkadian Life

Lefkadian Festivals and Events

One of the best ways to immerse yourself in Lefkadian culture is by attending one of the island's many festivals. I was lucky enough to visit during the International Folklore Festival in August, which brings together performers from all over the world.

Coordinates: The main events take place in Lefkada Town at (38.833333, 20.707500).

Address: Lefkada Town, Lefkada, Greece

Phone: +30 26450 22510

Price Range: Free to attend, though some events may have a small entry fee.

The festival is a vibrant celebration of music, dance, and tradition, with nightly performances in the town's main square. The atmosphere was electric, and I found myself swept up in the energy of the dancers and musicians. It was a wonderful way to connect with the island's rich cultural heritage.

Art and Craft Workshops

For a more hands-on cultural experience, I signed up for a pottery workshop in the village of Karya. The workshop was held in a small studio, where a local artist guided us through the process of creating traditional Lefkadian ceramics.

Coordinates: The workshop studio is located at (38.747117, 20.633064).

Address: Karya, Lefkada, Greece

Phone: +30 26450 41250

Price Range: Workshops start at around €30 per session.

Website: KaryaPottery.com

Working with clay was both challenging and therapeutic, and by the end of the session, I had crafted my very own Lefkadian vase. It's a unique souvenir that I'll treasure forever, and it gave me a deeper appreciation for the island's artisanal traditions.

Visiting Local Villages: Karya and Vasiliki

Exploring Lefkada's local villages offers a glimpse into the island's traditional way of life. Karya, with its stone houses and picturesque squares, is a perfect example of this. I spent an afternoon wandering through the village, visiting the Folklore Museum, and enjoying a leisurely lunch in one of the tavernas.

Coordinates: Karya is located at (38.747117, 20.633064).

Address: Karya, Lefkada, Greece

Phone: +30 26450 41989

Price Range: Museum entry is around €2.

Website: Search for Karya Folklore Museum.

Vasiliki, on the other hand, is a bustling village with a lively harbor. It's a great place to relax and watch the boats come and go. I particularly enjoyed an evening stroll along the waterfront, where I stumbled upon a small fish market selling the day's catch.

Music and Dance: The Sounds of Lefkada

Music and dance are at the heart of Lefkadian culture. I attended a live music performance at a local taverna in Lefkada Town, where a group of musicians played traditional Greek instruments like the bouzouki. The music was soulful, and soon enough, the whole room was clapping along and even joining in the dancing.

Coordinates: The taverna is located at (38.832711, 20.707788).

Address: Lefkada Town, Lefkada, Greece

Phone: +30 26450 24315

Price Range: No cover charge, though it's polite to order food or drinks.

Website: Local tavernas in Lefkada Town.

The experience was joyous and infectious, a true reflection of the island's spirit. Whether you're a seasoned dancer or just want to tap your feet to the rhythm, Lefkada's music scene is sure to captivate you.

Traditional Greek Cooking Classes

One of the highlights of my trip was taking a traditional Greek cooking class in the village of Vasiliki. The class was held in a family-run taverna, where we learned how to prepare classic dishes like moussaka, tzatziki, and baklava.

Coordinates: The taverna is located at (38.621469, 20.609801).

Address: Vasiliki, Lefkada, Greece

Phone: +30 26450 31167

Price Range: Classes start at around €50 per person.

Website: Search for cooking classes in Vasiliki.

The hands-on experience was both educational and fun, and the best part was sitting down to enjoy the meal we had prepared. Cooking with fresh, local ingredients gave me a new appreciation for Greek cuisine, and I've since tried to recreate some of the recipes at home.

Religious Sites and Pilgrimage

Lefkada is home to several important religious sites, the most notable being the Monastery of Faneromeni. Perched on a hill overlooking Lefkada Town, the monastery is a place of peace and spirituality. I visited during the Feast of the Dormition of the Virgin Mary in August, one of the most significant religious celebrations on the island.

Coordinates: The monastery is located at (38.837248, 20.683796).

Address: Faneromeni, Lefkada, Greece

Phone: +30 26450 21523

Price Range: Free to enter, donations appreciated.

Website: Search for Faneromeni Monastery.

The atmosphere during the feast was solemn yet festive, with locals and pilgrims gathering to pay their respects. The monastery's museum offers a fascinating insight into the island's religious history, and the views from the hilltop are simply breathtaking.

In conclusion, my time in Lefkada was filled with rich experiences that went beyond the typical tourist activities. From exploring the island at my own pace to immersing myself in its cultural traditions, Lefkada left a lasting impression on me. Whether you're seeking adventure, relaxation, or a deeper connection with Greek culture, Lefkada offers something for everyone.

Chapter 10

Shopping in Lefkada – From Souvenirs to Local Crafts

Best Markets and Boutiques

Shopping in Lefkada is a delightful experience, where the charm of the island extends even to its markets and boutiques. Strolling through Lefkada Town, I was amazed by the variety of shops, each offering something unique. One of my favorite spots was Agora Market in Lefkada Town, a bustling marketplace where you can find everything from fresh produce to handmade crafts. It's located at 38.8303° N, 20.7003° E and is open daily from 8:00 AM to 2:00 PM.

Another gem is the Melissa Boutique, situated at Lefkada 31100. This boutique offers a beautiful selection of clothes, jewelry, and accessories, all crafted by local designers. The atmosphere here is incredibly welcoming, and the staff are always eager to share the stories behind the products. The prices range from €20 to €150, depending on what you're looking for.

Phone: +30 26450 22311

Website: www.melissaboutique.gr

One evening, as I was wandering around, I stumbled upon Ekklisaki, a tiny boutique that specializes in religious icons and other spiritual items. The owner, a kind elderly lady, explained the history and significance of each piece with such passion. You can find it at 38.8303° N, 20.7016° E, and it's open from 9:00 AM to 8:00 PM.

What to Buy: Local Products and Artifacts

If you're looking to bring home a piece of Lefkada, there's no shortage of local products and artifacts that capture the essence of the island. One of the most iconic items is Lefkadian embroidery, known as "Karsaniko." This traditional craft originates from the village of Karya, where skilled artisans weave intricate designs using techniques passed down through generations. I picked up a small tablecloth for around €25 from a local shop in Karya.

Another must-buy is Lefkadian honey, particularly the thyme variety, which is harvested from the wild thyme bushes that grow abundantly on the island. You can find jars of this golden nectar in most markets and shops, with prices ranging from €8 to €15. I bought mine from a roadside stall near 38.7745° N, 20.6778° E on my way to Egremni Beach.

Address: Honey & More, Lefkada 31100

Contact: +30 26450 91234

One of my personal favorites is the Lefkadian wine, specifically the "Vertzami" red wine. The local wineries produce this wine using a grape variety unique to the island, resulting in a flavor that is rich and full-bodied. I visited Siflogo Winery in Sfakiotes (Latitude: 38.8001° N, Longitude: 20.7057° E) and had the pleasure of tasting their wines. Bottles are reasonably priced, ranging from €10 to €30.

Shopping for Fashion and Jewelry

Lefkada may not be Milan or Paris, but it certainly holds its own when it comes to fashion and jewelry. The island has several boutiques that offer trendy clothing and exquisite jewelry, often handcrafted by local artisans.

Vassiliki's Closet in Lefkada Town is a boutique that caught my eye. They have a great selection of summer dresses, beachwear, and accessories that are perfect for the island's vibe. The jewelry here is a mix of modern and traditional styles, with prices ranging from €15 for a simple bracelet to €100 for more elaborate pieces.

Address: Vassiliki's Closet, Lefkada 31100

Contact: +30 26450 21678

Opening hours: 10:00 AM - 9:00 PM

For something truly unique, Klio Creations in Nidri offers handmade jewelry crafted from materials like silver, leather, and semi-precious stones. The owner,

Klio, is a talented artist who takes pride in her work, and each piece is a reflection of her love for the island. I couldn't resist buying a necklace that featured a small silver pendant shaped like the island itself, priced at €45.

Lefkadian Wine and Olive Oil

One cannot leave Lefkada without indulging in its wine and olive oil. These products are not only a staple in the local diet but also make for wonderful gifts and souvenirs. As mentioned earlier, Vertzami wine is a must-try, and if you're interested in exploring more, I recommend visiting Lefkas Earth Winery in the village of Sfakiotes.

Coordinates: 38.7986° N, 20.7081° E

Opening hours: 11:00 AM - 7:00 PM

Price range: €12 - €30 per bottle

Website: www.lefkasearth.gr

When it comes to olive oil, Lefkada is renowned for its extra virgin olive oil, which has a rich, fruity flavor with a slight peppery finish. The Karya Cooperative produces some of the best olive oil on the island, which you can purchase at their shop in Karya village. A 500ml bottle costs around €7, and trust me, it's worth every cent.

Unique Souvenirs and Gifts

For those looking to bring home something truly special, Lefkada offers a variety of unique souvenirs and gifts that go beyond the usual tourist fare. One such item is the Lefkadian spoon sweets, which are traditional preserves made from fruits like grapes, figs, and kumquats. I bought a jar of grape spoon sweet from a small shop in Sivota for €5, and it was a hit with my friends back home.

Another unique gift idea is the Lefkadian sea salt harvested from the salt pans in the island's lagoons. This natural sea salt is rich in minerals and adds a wonderful flavor to any dish. You can find it at local markets, with prices starting at €3 for a small bag.

Lastly, don't miss out on the handmade ceramics produced by local artists. These beautiful pieces often feature designs inspired by the sea and the island's natural beauty. I purchased a small ceramic bowl with a blue wave pattern for €15 from a shop in Lefkada Town, located at 38.8310° N, 20.7025° E.

How to Bargain Like a Local

Bargaining isn't as common in Greece as it is in other Mediterranean countries, but there's still some room for negotiation, especially in the markets and with smaller vendors. The key is to be polite and respectful. I've found that a friendly chat with the shopkeeper can often lead to a small discount, particularly if you're buying multiple items.

For example, when I was purchasing a few bottles of olive oil and some ceramics, I managed to get a 10% discount simply by striking up a conversation with the shop owner and showing genuine interest in the products. It's also helpful to pay in cash, as many small businesses prefer it over credit cards.

Chapter 11

Nightlife and Entertainment – Enjoying the Island After Dark

Best Bars and Clubs in Lefkada Town

Lefkada may not be the party island that Mykonos is, but it still has a vibrant nightlife that caters to a wide range of tastes. In Lefkada Town, you'll find a variety of bars and clubs where you can enjoy a night out.

Vivarium Wine Bar is one of my favorite spots. It's located right in the heart of Lefkada Town at 38.8298° N, 20.7019° E. This cozy wine bar has an impressive selection of Greek wines, including some from Lefkada itself. The atmosphere is relaxed, making it a perfect place to start your evening. A glass of wine here ranges from €5 to €12.

Another popular spot is Milos Orlof. This beach bar is right on Gyra Beach and has a laid-back vibe during the day but turns into a lively spot in the evening.

They often have live DJs, and the cocktails are fantastic. I remember spending an entire evening here, sipping on mojitos and watching the sunset. Drinks are reasonably priced, with cocktails ranging from €8 to €12.

For those looking to dance the night away, Karma Club in Nidri is the place to be. This is one of the few clubs on the island that stays open until the early hours of the morning. With its energetic vibe and international DJs, it's a great place to let loose. Entry is usually free, but expect to pay around €10 for cocktails.

Coordinates: 38.7192° N, 20.7117° E

Opening hours: 11:00 PM - 4:00 AM

Live Music and Cultural Performances

Lefkada is known for its rich cultural heritage, and this extends to its nightlife as well. Many venues across the island offer live music, ranging from traditional Greek music to contemporary performances. One of the highlights of my trip was attending a live bouzouki performance at Café Mylos in Lefkada Town. The music was soulful, and the atmosphere was intimate, making it a memorable experience. The café is located at 38.8287° N, 20.7023° E, and there's no cover charge, although it's polite to order at least a drink or two.

Another great spot for live music is De Facto Bar in Nidri. They host regular live music nights featuring local bands and solo artists. The music varies from jazz to rock, and the ambiance is always lively. It's located at 38.7189° N, 20.7130° E, and the drinks are reasonably priced at around €7 for a cocktail.

Contact:

De Facto Bar, Nidri 31084

Phone: +30 26450 92345

Nighttime Beach Parties

One of the things I love about Lefkada is its beach parties. These events are usually held during the summer months and are a great way to experience the island's nightlife in a more relaxed setting. Kalamitsi Beach is a popular spot for these parties, where you can dance on the sand under the stars. The parties usually start around 10:00 PM and go on until the early hours of the morning. There's no entry fee, but you'll want to bring some cash for drinks.

Coordinates: 38.7711° N, 20.5869° E

Another beach known for its vibrant nighttime scene is Kathisma Beach. During the day, it's a tranquil spot for sunbathing, but at night, it transforms into a lively venue with music, dancing, and beach bars serving up cocktails. I attended a full moon party here once, and it was an unforgettable experience.

Where to Watch the Sunset

Watching the sunset in Lefkada is a magical experience, and there are several spots on the island that offer spectacular views. Cape Lefkatas, located at the southern tip of the island, is one of the best places to catch the sunset. The cliffs here are breathtaking, and as the sun dips below the horizon, the sky is painted with hues of orange, pink, and purple. It's a bit of a drive to get there, but the view is worth it.

Coordinates: 38.6014° N, 20.5421° E

Another favorite spot of mine is Agios Ioannis Beach. The beach itself is stunning, and the windmills along the shore add a unique touch to the sunset view. It's a quieter spot, making it perfect for a peaceful evening. I often brought a bottle of wine and some snacks to enjoy while watching the sunset here.

Quiet Evenings: Relaxing Nighttime Spots

For those who prefer a quieter evening, Lefkada has plenty of serene spots where you can unwind. One of my go-to places is Rachi Café in the village of Exanthia. Perched high on a hill, this café offers panoramic views of the island and the Ionian Sea. In the evening, the atmosphere is calm and peaceful, making it the perfect place to relax with a glass of wine. The café is located at 38.7604° N, 20.6392° E, and it's open until 11:00 PM.

Another peaceful spot is Kastro Maistro, a small bar located near the castle of Agia Mavra. This place has a cozy, laid-back vibe, and they serve some of the best cocktails on the island. The view of the castle lit up at night is stunning, and it's a great place to end the day.

Casino and Gaming Options

While Lefkada isn't known for its casinos, there are a few places where you can try your luck. Casino Corfu, located on the nearby island of Corfu, is the closest full-fledged casino. It's a bit of a trip, but if you're into gaming, it's worth the visit. They offer a variety of games, including roulette, blackjack, and slot machines.

Coordinates: 39.6211° N, 19.9237° E

Opening hours: 7:00 PM - 4:00 AM

Website: www.casinocorfu.gr

If you're looking for something closer, some of the larger hotels in Lefkada, like the Ionian Blue Hotel, have small gaming rooms where you can play slots and other electronic games. It's not a casino in the traditional sense, but it's a fun way to pass the time.

Chapter 12

Beaches of Lefkada – Sun, Sand, and Sea

Top Beaches to Visit

Lefkada is blessed with some of the most beautiful beaches in the world, each offering something unique. One of the top beaches that you absolutely must visit is Porto Katsiki. This iconic beach is often featured in travel magazines, and for good reason. The steep cliffs, turquoise waters, and fine white pebbles create a stunning landscape that's almost surreal. It's located on the southwestern coast of the island, at 38.6017° N, 20.5510° E. The beach is accessible via a series of steps, so be prepared for a bit of a hike, but once you're there, it's all worth it. Porto Katsiki is best visited early in the morning to avoid the crowds.

Another must-visit beach is Egremni Beach. Like Porto Katsiki, it's known for its dramatic cliffs and crystal-clear waters. What makes Egremni special is its length – it's a long, expansive beach, so even during peak season, you can find a spot to call your own. After the 2015 earthquake, access to the beach was limited, but as of my last visit, you can now reach it by boat, which adds to the adventure. The coordinates for Egremni are 38.6039° N, 20.5583° E.

For something a bit more lively, head to Kathisma Beach. This beach is one of the most popular on the island, thanks to its soft sand, beach bars, and amenities. It's a great place to spend the whole day, as you can easily grab a bite to eat or a drink without leaving the beach. The sunset views here are also fantastic, so plan to stay until evening. Kathisma is located at 38.7689° N, 20.6175° E.

Hidden Coves and Secluded Shores

If you're looking for a more secluded spot to relax, Lefkada has plenty of hidden coves and quiet beaches that offer peace and tranquility. One of my favorite hidden gems is Milos Beach, accessible only by foot or boat. The path to the beach starts from Agios Nikitas village and involves a bit of a hike, but once you arrive, you'll be rewarded with a pristine, quiet beach that feels like your own private paradise. The coordinates are 38.7852° N, 20.6092° E.

Another secluded spot is Gialos Beach. Located on the west coast of the island, Gialos is a long, sandy beach that's much less crowded than the more famous beaches. The road leading to the beach is narrow and winding, which deters many visitors, but if you're up for the drive, you'll find yourself in a peaceful, untouched setting. The coordinates for Gialos Beach are 38.6871° N, 20.5701° E.

Beach Clubs and Amenities

For those who enjoy a bit of luxury with their beach day, Lefkada has several beach clubs that offer sunbeds, umbrellas, and top-notch service. Copla Beach Bar at Kathisma Beach is one of the most popular, offering a chic, relaxed atmosphere with music, cocktails, and comfortable sunbeds. It's a bit pricey, with sunbeds costing around €20 for the day, but it's a great way to enjoy the beach in style. Copla is located at 38.7693° N, 20.6180° E.

Another great option is Deck Beach Bar at Agios Ioannis Beach. This beach club is more laid-back, with a focus on providing a peaceful, relaxing experience. The sunbeds are comfortable, and the food and drinks are excellent. It's a perfect spot to spend a lazy afternoon by the sea. The coordinates for Deck Beach Bar are 38.8364° N, 20.6795° E.

Family-Friendly Beaches

If you're traveling with kids, Lefkada has several beaches that are perfect for families. Nidri Beach is one such spot, offering shallow waters, soft sand, and plenty of amenities nearby. The beach is located in the popular resort town of Nidri, so you'll have easy access to restaurants, cafes, and shops. It's a great place to spend the day with the family, as the kids can safely play in the water while you relax on the shore. Nidri Beach is located at 38.7063° N, 20.7118° E.

Another family-friendly beach is Vasiliki Beach. Known for its calm waters, this beach is a favorite among families and windsurfing enthusiasts alike. The bay's gentle breezes make it a perfect spot for beginners to try out windsurfing or paddleboarding. The beach is lined with tavernas, so you can easily grab a meal or snack without leaving the beach. Vasiliki Beach is located at 38.6283° N, 20.6139° E.

Tips for Safe Swimming and Sunbathing

Lefkada's beaches are stunning, but it's important to stay safe while enjoying them. The island's west coast beaches, like Porto Katsiki and Egremni, are known for their strong currents, so always be cautious when swimming. Stick to the designated swimming areas, and if the sea looks rough, it's best to stay on the shore. I've seen waves come in unexpectedly strong, so it's always good to keep an eye on the water.

When it comes to sunbathing, remember that the sun in Greece can be very intense, especially during the summer months. Always apply a high-SPF sunscreen, wear a hat, and bring plenty of water to stay hydrated. Sunbeds and umbrellas are available at most of the popular beaches, but if you're heading to a more secluded spot, it's a good idea to bring your own shade.

Best Beaches for Water Sports

Lefkada is a paradise for water sports enthusiasts, offering a wide range of activities from windsurfing to snorkeling. Vasiliki Beach is one of the top spots on the island for windsurfing, thanks to its consistent afternoon winds known as "Eric." The bay is filled with windsurfers of all levels, and there are several schools where you can take lessons or rent equipment.

For snorkeling, Agiofili Beach near Vasiliki is a fantastic choice. The clear, calm waters here are perfect for exploring the underwater world, and you'll find plenty of fish and other marine life just a short swim from the shore. The coordinates for Agiofili Beach are 38.6226° N, 20.6113° E.

Another great spot for water sports is Mikros Gialos Beach in Rouda Bay. This beach is known for its calm, crystal-clear waters, making it ideal for kayaking and stand-up paddleboarding. You can rent equipment right on the beach, and the bay's protected waters ensure a smooth, enjoyable experience. Mikros Gialos is located at 38.6321° N, 20.6877° E.

Chapter 13

Health and Wellness – Relax and Rejuvenate

Spas and Wellness Centers

When I think back to my time in Lefkada, one of the most rejuvenating experiences was visiting the various spas and wellness centers scattered across the island. After days of exploring the island's rugged beauty, there's nothing quite like indulging in a bit of pampering.

Lefkas Earth Spa was one of my favorite spots. Nestled in the heart of Lefkada Town (38.8302° N, 20.7105° E), this spa is a sanctuary of calm. The moment I walked in, the gentle aroma of essential oils enveloped me, and I could feel my worries begin to melt away. I opted for a traditional Greek massage, a treatment that combines deep tissue massage with the healing properties of local herbs. The therapists here are incredibly skilled, and I left feeling completely renewed. The spa also offers facials, body scrubs, and a range of other treatments, all using organic, locally sourced products.

Opening hours: 10:00 AM - 8:00 PM

Address: K. Karamanli 10, Lefkada Town, 31100

Contact: +30 26450 25078

Price range: €50 - €150

Another gem is the Ionian Blue Spa Resort (38.7458° N, 20.6664° E), located on the east coast of the island. This luxurious resort boasts a full-service spa with stunning views of the Ionian Sea. I treated myself to a hot stone massage here, which was pure bliss. The spa also has a sauna, steam room, and a beautiful infinity pool where you can unwind after your treatments.

Opening hours: 9:00 AM - 7:00 PM

Address: Nikiana, Lefkada, 31100

Contact: +30 26450 93000

Price range: €60 - €200

Website: ionianblue.gr

Yoga and Meditation Retreats

For a more holistic wellness experience, Lefkada offers several yoga and meditation retreats that allow you to connect deeply with your inner self amidst the island's natural beauty.

I spent a weekend at the Inspire Yoga Retreat (38.7452° N, 20.6629° E) in Vassiliki, a picturesque village on the southern tip of the island. The retreat is set on a hillside overlooking the bay, and waking up to the sound of waves gently lapping the shore is a memory I'll cherish forever. The retreat offers daily yoga sessions, meditation classes, and workshops on mindfulness. The instructors were incredibly warm and welcoming, making it a perfect place for both beginners and experienced practitioners.

Opening hours: 7:00 AM - 9:00 PM (Retreat schedules vary)

Address: Vassiliki, Lefkada, 31082

Contact: +30 694 592 8168

Price range: €400 - €1500 (depending on the retreat duration)

Website: inspireyogaretreats.gr

Another retreat that caught my attention was the Odyssey Retreats (38.7631° N, 20.6457° E) located near Nidri. This retreat is more intimate, with personalized sessions that focus on both physical and spiritual well-being. I joined a group meditation session here, and the serene environment truly enhanced the experience. The retreat also offers detox programs, healing therapies, and organic meals tailored to your wellness journey.

Opening hours: 6:30 AM - 8:30 PM

Address: Nidri, Lefkada, 31100

Contact: +30 693 265 4002

Price range: €500 - €2000

Website: odysseyretreats.com

Natural Hot Springs and Baths

While Lefkada isn't as famous for hot springs as other parts of Greece, the island does have some natural baths that are perfect for a relaxing soak.

One such place is the Atherinos Baths near the village of Dragano (38.6989° N, 20.6234° E). This hidden gem is a local secret, and the water is rich in minerals believed to have healing properties. The baths are set in a tranquil environment, surrounded by lush greenery. Taking a dip here after a long day of hiking was incredibly soothing.

Opening hours: Always open

Address: Dragano, Lefkada, 31082

Healthy Eating and Organic Cafes

Healthy eating is easy on Lefkada, with numerous cafes and restaurants focusing on organic and locally sourced ingredients.

One of my favorite spots was Roots Organic Café (38.8305° N, 20.7099° E) in Lefkada Town. The café is bright and welcoming, with a menu full of nutritious options. I loved their smoothie bowls, packed with fresh fruit, nuts, and seeds, as well as their salads made with vegetables straight from local farms. They also offer vegan and gluten-free options, catering to all dietary preferences.

Opening hours: 8:00 AM - 6:00 PM

Address: Marinos Gerasimos 12, Lefkada Town, 31100

Contact: +30 26450 22388

Price range: €5 - €15

Another excellent place for a healthy meal is Elly's Place (38.8298° N, 20.7104° E), also in Lefkada Town. This cozy café specializes in organic coffee and plant-based dishes. I particularly enjoyed their avocado toast and the freshly pressed juices, which were perfect for a light lunch after a morning of exploring the town.

Opening hours: 7:30 AM - 5:00 PM

Address: Pl. Ethnikis Antistaseos 10, Lefkada Town, 31100

Contact: +30 26450 25123

Price range: €4 - €12

Website: ellysplace.gr

Fitness Centers and Gyms

Staying active while traveling is important to me, and Lefkada has several gyms and fitness centers where you can keep up with your workout routine.

Lefkada Fitness Club (38.8324° N, 20.7116° E) in Lefkada Town is a modern gym with a wide range of equipment. They offer day passes, which was perfect for me since I was just visiting. The gym is clean, well-maintained, and the staff were friendly and helpful. They also have group classes like spinning, aerobics, and Pilates, which I found to be a great way to mix up my workout routine.

Opening hours: 7:00 AM - 10:00 PM

Address: Filippa Panagou 2, Lefkada Town, 31100

Contact: +30 26450 26687

Price range: €7 for a day pass, €30 for a weekly pass

Another option is the Vassiliki Fitness Studio (38.7329° N, 20.6145° E) in Vassiliki. This smaller gym is ideal for those staying in the southern part of the island. It has all the basic equipment you need, and the atmosphere is friendly and relaxed. I enjoyed their yoga classes, which were held on a terrace overlooking the sea – an experience that combined fitness with the natural beauty of Lefkada.

Opening hours: 8:00 AM - 9:00 PM

Address: Vassiliki, Lefkada, 31082

Contact: +30 26450 31824

Price range: €5 - €10 per session

Wellness Resorts and Packages

For those looking to completely immerse themselves in wellness, Lefkada offers several resorts with comprehensive wellness packages.

Porto Galini Seaside Resort & Spa (38.7467° N, 20.6703° E) in Nikiana is a top choice for wellness enthusiasts. The resort is set in a beautiful location with its own private beach, and the wellness packages here are all-encompassing. I stayed here for three days and indulged in their "Detox & Rejuvenation" package, which included daily yoga sessions, detoxifying spa treatments, and meals designed to cleanse the body. The resort also offers fitness classes, guided meditation, and nature walks.

Opening hours: 24 hours (Resort services vary)

Address: Nikiana, Lefkada, 31100

Contact: +30 26450 93494

Price range: €200 - €500 per night

Website: portogalini.gr

Another luxurious option is the Ionian Sun Resort (38.7503° N, 20.6671° E) in Nikiana. This resort offers wellness retreats that focus on holistic health, with packages that include personalized fitness training, spa treatments, and nutrition consultations. The resort's serene setting, combined with its comprehensive wellness offerings, made my stay here deeply restorative.

Opening hours: 24 hours (Resort services vary)

Address: Nikiana, Lefkada, 31100

Contact: +30 26450 93111

Price range: €180 - €450 per night

Website: ioniansun.gr

Chapter 14

Day Trips and Excursions – Exploring Beyond Lefkada

Day Trip to Kefalonia

Lefkada is a wonderful base for exploring nearby islands, and one of the most memorable day trips I took was to the stunning island of Kefalonia.

To get to Kefalonia, I took a ferry from Nidri (38.7212° N, 20.7105° E) to the port of Fiskardo (38.4617° N, 20.5766° E) on the northern tip of Kefalonia. The ferry ride takes about an hour and a half, and the views along the way are breathtaking, with the turquoise waters of the Ionian Sea sparkling under the sun.

Fiskardo is a charming village, with pastel-colored houses lining the harbor and fishing boats bobbing gently in the water. I spent some time wandering through the narrow streets, browsing the local shops, and enjoying a coffee at one of the waterfront cafes. Fiskardo has a relaxed, laid-back vibe that made me feel like I had stepped back in time.

One of the highlights of my trip to Kefalonia was visiting Myrtos Beach (38.3722° N, 20.5306° E), which is often cited as one of the most beautiful beaches in Greece. The beach is about a 40-minute drive from Fiskardo, and the road leading down to it offers some incredible views. Myrtos is a stunning crescent of white sand and pebbles, with cliffs rising steeply behind it. The water here is a vivid shade of blue, almost too beautiful to be real. I spent the afternoon swimming, sunbathing, and simply soaking in the beauty of the surroundings.

Another must-visit spot on Kefalonia is Assos Village (38.3652° N, 20.5225° E), a picturesque village nestled on a narrow isthmus that connects the main island to the Assos Peninsula. The village is incredibly photogenic, with its colorful houses, quaint streets, and the imposing ruins of the Venetian castle perched on the hill above. I enjoyed a leisurely lunch at one of the tavernas by the sea, savoring fresh seafood and local specialties.

Kefalonia is a large island with much to offer, so while a day trip gives you a taste of its beauty, I would recommend spending a few days if you have the time.

Ferry schedule: 9:00 AM - 6:00 PM (Check specific times)

Ferry price: €20 - €50 (round trip)

Website: lefkadaferries.gr

Discovering Ithaca

Ithaca, the legendary home of Odysseus, is another fantastic day trip option from Lefkada. This island, known for its rugged landscapes and unspoiled beauty, is perfect for those looking to explore a quieter, more authentic side of the Ionian Islands.

I took a ferry from Vassiliki (38.6325° N, 20.6172° E) to the port of Piso Aetos (38.3754° N, 20.7169° E) on Ithaca. The journey takes just under an hour, and as you approach Ithaca, the island's mountainous terrain comes into view, creating a dramatic and inviting landscape.

One of the first places I visited was Vathi (38.3678° N, 20.7183° E), the island's capital. Vathi is a charming town built around a deep natural harbor, with red-roofed houses cascading down the hillsides. The town has a tranquil atmosphere, and I loved strolling along the waterfront, exploring the narrow streets, and visiting the small but interesting Archaeological Museum of Ithaca, where you can learn about the island's ancient history.

From Vathi, I took a short drive to Kioni (38.4606° N, 20.7103° E), a picturesque village on the northeast coast of the island. Kioni is incredibly scenic, with its traditional houses, fishing boats in the harbor, and lush green hills surrounding it. I spent a relaxing afternoon here, enjoying a meal at a seaside taverna and taking a dip in the crystal-clear waters.

For those interested in history and mythology, a visit to Homer's School (38.3897° N, 20.6683° E) is a must. This ancient site is believed to be the location of Odysseus' palace, and while the ruins are not extensive, the site offers stunning views of the surrounding countryside and the sea.

Ferry schedule: 8:00 AM - 7:00 PM (Check specific times)

Ferry price: €15 - €40 (round trip)

Website: ithacaferries.gr

Sailing to Paxos and Antipaxos

One of the most unforgettable experiences I had while staying in Lefkada was a sailing trip to the islands of Paxos and Antipaxos. These small islands, located just south of Corfu, are known for their stunning beaches and crystal-clear waters.

The trip started from the port of Lefkada Town (38.8302° N, 20.7105° E), where I boarded a catamaran for the day. The boat was spacious and comfortable, and as we set sail, I felt a sense of freedom and adventure that only being out on the open sea can provide.

Our first stop was Gaios (39.2021° N, 20.1837° E), the main town on Paxos. Gaios is a charming town with narrow streets, Venetian architecture, and a bustling harbor. I spent some time exploring the town, visiting the small shops, and enjoying a coffee at one of the cafes by the water.

After leaving Gaios, we sailed to Antipaxos (39.1764° N, 20.1933° E), a tiny island just a few kilometers south of Paxos. Antipaxos is famous for its beaches, and Vrika Beach (39.1687° N, 20.1925° E) is one of the most beautiful I've ever seen. The sand is white and powdery, and the water is so clear it's like swimming in a giant pool. I spent hours here, snorkeling and relaxing on the beach.

The trip also included a stop at the Blue Caves of Paxos (39.2053° N, 20.1389° E), a series of sea caves with stunning blue water that glows when the sunlight hits it. Exploring these caves by boat was a magical experience, and it was the perfect way to end the day.

Sailing schedule: 9:00 AM - 5:00 PM

Sailing price: €60 - €100 per person

Website: lefkadasailing.gr

Exploring the Mainland: Parga and Sivota

While the Ionian Islands are a paradise, the mainland opposite Lefkada also has its own charm, and a day trip to Parga and Sivota was a highlight of my travels.

Parga (39.2832° N, 20.4007° E) is a picturesque town on the Epirus coast, known for its colorful houses, beautiful beaches, and Venetian castle. The town has a lively atmosphere, with plenty of shops, cafes, and restaurants to explore. I particularly enjoyed visiting the Castle of Parga (39.2854° N, 20.4005° E), which offers panoramic views of the town and the Ionian Sea. The castle is well-preserved, and walking through its ancient walls, I could almost imagine what life was like here centuries ago.

After exploring Parga, I drove to Sivota (39.4072° N, 20.2463° E), a small village about 30 minutes away. Sivota is known for its stunning coastline, with hidden coves and crystal-clear waters. I took a boat tour to the nearby Blue Lagoon (39.4239° N, 20.2358° E), a secluded bay with some of the clearest water I've ever seen. Swimming in the Blue Lagoon was an incredible experience, and it's a spot I would highly recommend to anyone visiting the area.

If you're looking for a relaxing day trip that combines beautiful scenery, history, and some of the best beaches on the mainland, Parga and Sivota are excellent choices.

Address: Parga and Sivota, Epirus Region

Adventure Excursions: Kayaking and Rafting

For those seeking a bit of adventure, Lefkada and its surrounding areas offer fantastic opportunities for kayaking and rafting.

One of the most exciting experiences I had was a kayaking tour along the western coast of Lefkada. We started from Kathisma Beach (38.7597° N, 20.6144° E), one of the island's most beautiful beaches, and paddled along the coastline, exploring hidden caves and secluded coves. The water here is a stunning shade of blue, and the cliffs rising up from the sea create a dramatic backdrop. Our guide was knowledgeable and ensured we were all safe while still having fun. We even stopped at a small beach that's only accessible by boat, where we enjoyed a picnic lunch.

If you're up for a bit more adrenaline, rafting on the Acheron River (39.2239° N, 20.5637° E) on the mainland is an adventure not to be missed. The river is about an hour and a half drive from Lefkada, and it's known for its crystal-clear waters and lush green surroundings. The rafting route is suitable for beginners, but it still offers plenty of thrills as you navigate through small rapids and around bends in the river. The highlight for me was floating through the Acheron Springs (39.2224° N, 20.5665° E), where the water is so clear it's like floating on air.

Kayaking price: €50 - €80 per person

Rafting price: €40 - €60 per person

Website: lefkadaadventures.gr

Historical Tours and Archaeological Sites

For history buffs, the area around Lefkada offers a wealth of archaeological sites and historical tours that provide a glimpse into the region's rich past.

One of the most significant sites is the Ancient City of Nikopolis (39.0015° N, 20.7521° E), located near the town of Preveza, about 30 minutes from Lefkada. Nikopolis was founded by the Roman Emperor

Octavian in 31 BC to commemorate his victory at the Battle of Actium. Walking through the ruins of this once-great city, I could feel the weight of history around me. The site is extensive, with remains of temples, theaters, and the impressive walls that once protected the city. There's also a small museum on-site where you can see artifacts uncovered during excavations.

Another fascinating site is the Necromanteion of Acheron (39.1744° N, 20.5567° E), an ancient Greek temple dedicated to the god of the underworld, Hades. The site is located near the Acheron River and was believed to be the gateway to the underworld. Visiting the Necromanteion was an eerie but fascinating experience, as you walk through dark corridors and chambers where ancient rituals were performed.

For those interested in more recent history, a visit to the Castle of Santa Maura (38.8316° N, 20.7129° E) in Lefkada Town is a must. This Venetian fortress was built in the 14th century and played a crucial role in defending the island from invaders. The castle is well-preserved, and the views from the top are stunning, offering a panoramic view of the town and the surrounding sea.

Historical tour price: €10 - €20 per person

Website: lefkadaarchaeology.gr

Chapter 15

Lefkada for Families – A Guide to Kid-Friendly Fun

Top Attractions for Families

Lefkada is a fantastic destination for families, offering a wide range of attractions that are sure to delight kids of all ages.

One of the top attractions for families is Lefkada Water Park (38.7261° N, 20.6474° E) located in Nidri. This small but fun water park is perfect for a day of family fun. The park has several water slides, a lazy river, and a large pool where kids can splash around to their heart's content. There's also a shallow area for younger children, ensuring that everyone in the family can have a good time. My kids loved the adrenaline-pumping slides, while I enjoyed lounging by the pool with a cool drink.

Opening hours: 10:00 AM - 6:00 PM (summer months)

Address: Nidri, Lefkada, 31100

Contact: +30 26450 92567

Price range: €15 - €25 per person

Another must-visit spot is the Lefkada Puppet Theater (38.8309° N, 20.7096° E) in Lefkada Town. This charming theater offers puppet shows that are both entertaining and educational, bringing to life Greek myths and stories. The shows are in Greek, but even if you don't speak the language, the expressive puppets and lively performances make it easy to follow along. It's a great way for kids to learn about Greek culture in a fun and engaging way.

Opening hours: Showtimes vary

Address: Lefkada Town, 31100

Contact: +30 26450 22697

Price range: €5 - €10 per person

Kid-Friendly Restaurants and Cafes

Finding kid-friendly places to eat in Lefkada is easy, as many restaurants cater to families with young children.

One of our favorite spots was Tree House Restaurant (38.8294° N, 20.7103° E) in Lefkada Town. This quirky restaurant is designed to look like a giant tree house, with wooden beams, hanging plants, and a playful atmosphere that kids love. The menu features a variety of Greek and Mediterranean dishes, and they have a special kids' menu with smaller portions and kid-friendly options like spaghetti, pizza, and grilled chicken. The staff are very friendly and go out of their way to make sure kids are happy.

Opening hours: 12:00 PM - 11:00 PM

Address: Lefkada Town, 31100

Contact: +30 26450 22567

Price range: €10 - €20 per person

Another great option is Captain's Corner (38.7312° N, 20.6485° E) in Nidri. This family-friendly taverna is right on the waterfront, with outdoor seating that offers beautiful views of the harbor. The menu is extensive, with plenty of options for both adults and kids. My children loved the fresh fish and chips, while my partner and I enjoyed traditional Greek dishes like moussaka and souvlaki. The taverna also has a play area where kids can burn off some energy while waiting for their food.

Opening hours: 11:00 AM - 11:00 PM

Address: Nidri, Lefkada, 31100

Contact: +30 26450 92456

Price range: €8 - €18 per person

Family Beaches and Pools

Lefkada is known for its stunning beaches, and there are plenty that are perfect for families with young children.

Agios Ioannis Beach (38.8501° N, 20.7002° E) is one of the most family-friendly beaches on the island. The beach has shallow waters, making it safe for kids to swim and play. There are also plenty of amenities nearby, including cafes, restaurants, and shops, so you can easily spend the whole day here. My kids had a blast building sandcastles and splashing in the gentle waves, while I enjoyed lounging under the shade of an umbrella.

Opening hours: Always open

Address: Agios Ioannis, Lefkada, 31100

Another great beach for families is Kathisma Beach (38.7597° N, 20.6144° E). While the main part of the beach can get quite busy, there are quieter sections where families can relax and enjoy the sun. The beach is well-organized, with sunbeds and umbrellas available for rent, and there are plenty of tavernas nearby where you can grab a bite to eat. The water here is a bit deeper, so it's better for older kids who are confident swimmers.

Opening hours: Always open

Address: Kathisma, Lefkada, 31080

Educational and Fun Activities

Lefkada offers a variety of educational and fun activities that are perfect for families looking to combine learning with play.

One of the best educational experiences we had was visiting the Lefkada Olive Oil Museum (38.7494° N, 20.6201° E) in the village of Syvros. The museum is housed in a traditional olive mill, and it offers a fascinating look at the history of olive oil production on the island. Kids can learn about how olives are harvested, pressed, and turned into oil, and there's even a tasting room where you can sample different types of olive oil. The museum is very interactive, with hands-on exhibits that kept my children engaged and interested.

Opening hours: 9:00 AM - 5:00 PM

Address: Syvros, Lefkada, 31082

Contact: +30 26450 61985

Price range: €3 - €5 per person

Another fun and educational activity is a visit to the Sea Turtle Rescue Center (38.7301° N, 20.6485° E) in Nidri. The center is dedicated to rescuing and rehabilitating injured sea turtles, and it's a great place for kids to learn about marine life and conservation efforts. The staff are passionate about their work, and they offer guided tours that are both informative and engaging. My children were thrilled to see the turtles up close and learn about the important work being done to protect these amazing creatures.

Opening hours: 10:00 AM - 6:00 PM

Address: Nidri, Lefkada, 31100

Contact: +30 26450 92230

Price range: €5 - €10 per person

Adventure Parks and Playgrounds

For a bit of outdoor fun, Lefkada has several adventure parks and playgrounds that are perfect for families.

Lefkada Adventure Park (38.8322° N, 20.7103° E) in Lefkada Town is a great place for kids to burn off some energy. The park has a variety of activities, including climbing walls, zip lines, and obstacle courses. My kids had a blast navigating the ropes course, which is designed to be challenging but safe for children. The park also has a playground area for younger kids, as well as picnic tables where you can relax and enjoy a snack.

Opening hours: 10:00 AM - 8:00 PM

Address: Lefkada Town, 31100

Contact: +30 26450 22578

Price range: €10 - €20 per person

Another fun spot is Vassiliki Playground (38.7312° N, 20.6155° E) in Vassiliki. This small playground is located near the beach, and it's a great place for younger kids to play while parents relax nearby. The playground is well-maintained and has a variety of equipment, including swings, slides, and climbing frames. It's also close to several cafes and restaurants, so you can easily grab a coffee or a bite to eat while keeping an eye on the kids.

Opening hours: Always open

Address: Vassiliki, Lefkada, 31082

Tips for Traveling with Children

Traveling with children can be a bit challenging, but with a little planning, it can also be incredibly rewarding. Here are a few tips that I found helpful during our family trip to Lefkada:

Pack Snacks: Lefkada has plenty of great places to eat, but it's always a good idea to have some snacks on hand for when hunger strikes. I packed a variety of healthy snacks like fruit, nuts, and granola bars, which helped keep my kids happy and fueled during our outings.

Plan for Downtime: While it's tempting to try and see everything, it's important to plan for some downtime, especially with younger kids. We made sure to include some beach days and leisurely afternoons in our itinerary, which gave everyone a chance to relax and recharge.

Bring Sunscreen: The sun in Lefkada can be quite strong, so be sure to pack plenty of sunscreen and apply it regularly. I also brought along hats and lightweight clothing to protect my kids from the sun.

Choose Kid-Friendly Accommodations: When booking accommodations, look for places that cater to families, with amenities like cribs, high chairs, and play areas. We stayed at a family-friendly hotel in Nidri that had a kids' pool and a playground, which made our stay much more enjoyable.

Involve the Kids in Planning: I found that involving my kids in the planning process made them more excited about the trip. We looked at photos of Lefkada together and talked about the places we wanted to visit, which helped build anticipation and made the trip more fun for everyone.

Traveling with children may require a bit more effort, but the memories you create together are worth it. Lefkada is a fantastic destination for families, offering a perfect blend of adventure, relaxation, and cultural experiences that will create lasting memories for both kids and adults.

Chapter 16

Budget Travel – Enjoying Lefkada on a Shoestring

Traveling to Lefkada on a budget doesn't mean missing out on the island's beauty and charm. In fact, some of the most memorable experiences I've had on this Greek gem were inexpensive or completely free. From finding budget-friendly places to stay to enjoying delicious street food, here's how you can enjoy Lefkada without breaking the bank.

Budget-Friendly Accommodation

Finding affordable accommodation in Lefkada is easier than you might think. I remember staying in a quaint little guesthouse in Lefkada Town that offered comfort and convenience without the hefty price tag. Guesthouses and budget hotels are scattered across the island, and they provide a cozy atmosphere perfect for travelers who prefer a more authentic experience.

My Favorite Budget Stay: The guesthouse I stayed at was called "Villa Olga Lounge Hotel". It's a lovely place located in Lygia, just a short drive from Lefkada Town. The rooms were clean, comfortable, and came with a small kitchenette – perfect for preparing your own meals if you're really trying to save. The price for a night was around €40-€60, depending on the season.

Address: Lygia, Lefkada, Greece

Coordinates: 38.7864° N, 20.6976° E

Contact: +30 2645 071400

Price Range: €40-€60 per night

Website: villaolga.gr

For solo travelers, hostels like "Ionion Star Hotel" offer dormitory-style accommodation where you can share a room with other travelers, often costing less than €30 per night. It's a great way to meet new people while keeping costs low.

Address: Lefkada Town, Lefkada, Greece

Coordinates: 38.8324° N, 20.7052° E

Contact: +30 2645 024200

Price Range: €25-€35 per night

Website: ionionstar.com

Affordable Dining and Street Food

Lefkada is a paradise for food lovers, and you don't have to dine at high-end restaurants to enjoy its culinary delights. The island is dotted with affordable eateries where you can taste authentic Greek dishes.

One of my favorite places for a budget meal is "Pita Gyros" in Lefkada Town. For just €3-€5, you can grab a delicious gyro packed with freshly cooked meat, vegetables, and tzatziki sauce. It's filling, flavorful, and won't hurt your wallet.

Address: Golemi 5, Lefkada Town, Lefkada, Greece

Coordinates: 38.8325° N, 20.7039° E

Contact: +30 2645 023218

Price Range: €3-€7 per meal

Another spot I love is "Kafeneio O Platanos" in the village of Karya. This traditional taverna serves hearty Greek meals for under €10. I particularly enjoyed their moussaka, which was rich, comforting, and only cost around €8.

Address: Karya, Lefkada, Greece

Coordinates: 38.7402° N, 20.6400° E

Contact: +30 2645 041235

Price Range: €5-€10 per meal

For something sweet, don't miss out on "Lefkadian sweets". You can find bakeries offering treats like baklava or kataifi for just a couple of euros. One bakery I frequently visited was "Thymari" in Lefkada Town, where the staff were always friendly and the pastries were fresh out of the oven.

Address: Filippa Panagou 5, Lefkada Town, Lefkada, Greece

Coordinates: 38.8331° N, 20.7029° E

Contact: +30 2645 023481

Price Range: €2-€5 per pastry

Free and Low-Cost Attractions

One of the best things about Lefkada is that many of its most beautiful sights are free to enjoy. I spent countless hours exploring the island's natural wonders without spending a cent.

Beaches: Lefkada's beaches are legendary, and they're all free to visit. My personal favorite is Porto Katsiki. The drive there is a bit of an adventure, winding through the hills, but the sight of that turquoise water is absolutely worth it.

Coordinates: 38.6014° N, 20.5565° E

Address: Porto Katsiki Beach, Lefkada, Greece

Price: Free

Nidri Waterfalls: Another free attraction I loved was the Nidri Waterfalls. It's a short hike through lush greenery to reach the falls, and the sound of the water rushing down is incredibly peaceful. I even dipped my feet in the cool water – a refreshing treat on a hot day.

Coordinates: 38.7225° N, 20.7057° E

Address: Dimosari Waterfalls, Nidri, Lefkada, Greece

Price: Free

Lefkada Town: Just wandering around Lefkada Town is a joy in itself. The narrow streets, colorful buildings, and lively squares make for a perfect afternoon stroll. And if you're interested in history, the Archaeological Museum of Lefkada offers entry for just a few euros.

Address: Aggelou Sikelianou Square, Lefkada Town, Greece

Coordinates: 38.8343° N, 20.7037° E

Price: €3 per person

Opening Hours: Tuesday-Sunday, 08:30-15:30

Money-Saving Tips and Tricks

Saving money in Lefkada isn't hard if you know where to look and how to plan. One trick I often used was shopping at local markets. The Lefkada Town Market is filled with fresh produce, bread, cheese, and olives, all at prices lower than what you'd find in supermarkets. I'd often grab a few items and have a picnic by the beach.

Address: Lefkada Town, Lefkada, Greece

Coordinates: 38.8340° N, 20.7011° E

Opening Hours: Daily, 07:00-13:00

Price Range: Various, generally low-cost

Another tip is to travel during the shoulder seasons – late spring or early autumn. Prices for accommodation and flights drop significantly, and the weather is still warm enough to enjoy the beaches. Plus, you'll avoid the summer crowds.

Using public transportation instead of renting a car can also save you money. Lefkada has a decent bus system that can take you to most major destinations on the island. A bus ride from Lefkada Town to Porto Katsiki, for example, costs around €3.

Lastly, don't hesitate to haggle at local markets and with vendors for souvenirs. I found that many sellers are open to negotiating, especially if you're buying multiple items.

Public Transportation and Walking Tours

Getting around Lefkada on a budget is entirely possible with the island's public transportation and your own two feet. The KTEL Lefkada buses are reliable and cover most of the island. A single ticket usually costs between €2 and €5, depending on the distance. I used the bus system frequently, especially when I didn't want to deal with the hassle of parking.

Contact: +30 2645 022364

Price Range: €2-€5 per ticket

Website: ktel-lefkadas.gr

One of the best ways to see Lefkada Town is by foot. I joined a walking tour with a local guide who shared stories about the island's history and culture. The tour cost about €10 and lasted two hours, taking us through the town's old quarters, past historical landmarks, and ending with a coffee at a local café.

Traveling on a Budget: What You Need to Know

Traveling on a budget in Lefkada is entirely feasible with a bit of planning. Start by setting a daily budget – I aimed for around €50 per day, which covered accommodation, food, and activities. By prioritizing what you want to spend on, like a nice dinner or a guided tour, you can easily balance your expenses.

I also recommend carrying some cash, as not all places accept cards, especially in more rural areas. However, most towns have ATMs if you need them.

Planning your itinerary to include free activities, like beach days or hiking, can significantly reduce your daily costs. And don't forget about the little things, like refilling your water bottle at public fountains instead of buying bottled water – it's a small saving, but it adds up over time.

Traveling light, packing essentials like snacks for the day, and embracing the local way of life will not only save you money but also give you a more authentic Lefkadian experience.

Chapter 17

Solo Traveler's Guide – Exploring Lefkada Alone

Traveling solo in Lefkada was one of the most liberating experiences I've ever had. There's something incredibly peaceful about exploring the island at your own pace, without any distractions. Whether you're seeking solitude or hoping to meet new people, Lefkada is a great place for solo adventurers.

Why Lefkada is Perfect for Solo Travelers

Lefkada is an ideal destination for solo travelers because of its friendly locals, safe environment, and manageable size. The island is big enough to keep you entertained but small enough that you can easily navigate it on your own. During my solo trip, I never felt overwhelmed or out of place.

One of the best parts about traveling solo in Lefkada is the freedom to do exactly what you want. If you're a beach lover, you can spend your days hopping from one stunning shoreline to the next. If you're into history, you can take your time exploring ancient ruins and museums without feeling rushed. The island's laid-back vibe makes it easy to relax and enjoy the moment.

Safety Tips and Precautions

Safety was one of my primary concerns when I first decided to travel solo, but Lefkada quickly put me at ease. The island is known for its low crime rate, and I felt comfortable walking around alone, even at night. However, it's always wise to take a few precautions.

First, I made sure to keep my valuables secure. I used a money belt to carry my cash, cards, and passport, and I left unnecessary items in my hotel safe. When exploring remote areas or hiking alone, I always informed someone at my accommodation where I was going and when I expected to return.

Staying in well-populated areas and avoiding deserted places after dark is a good rule of thumb. In the rare event that you need assistance, locals are generally very helpful, and most speak at least basic English.

Solo-Friendly Accommodation

Finding accommodation as a solo traveler in Lefkada is straightforward. I stayed at "Nirikos Hotel" in Lefkada Town, which was perfect for solo travelers. The rooms were modest but comfortable, and the location was central, making it easy to explore the town on foot. I particularly appreciated the friendly staff, who gave me great tips on where to go and what to see.

Address: Lefkada Town, Lefkada, Greece

Coordinates: 38.8336° N, 20.7006° E

Contact: +30 2645 022300

Price Range: €40-€60 per night

Website: nirikos.gr

Another option for solo travelers is to stay in a hostel, where you can meet other travelers. "George's Place" in Nidri is a popular choice, offering dormitory-style rooms that are both affordable and social. The hostel also organizes group activities like BBQ nights and boat trips, which are perfect for meeting new people.

Address: Nidri, Lefkada, Greece

Coordinates: 38.7167° N, 20.7045° E

Contact: +30 2645 092080

Price Range: €20-€30 per night

Meeting People and Making Friends

Traveling alone doesn't mean you have to be lonely. In Lefkada, I found it easy to strike up conversations with fellow travelers and locals alike. One of the best places to meet people is at the beach – everyone is in a relaxed mood, and it's common to see groups playing volleyball or enjoying a drink together.

Joining a group tour is another great way to meet like-minded travelers. I took a sailing tour around the island with "Sail Lefkas", and it was an amazing experience. Not only did I get to see Lefkada from the water, but I also made friends with a group of travelers from all over the world.

Address: Vlicho Bay, Lefkada, Greece

Coordinates: 38.6910° N, 20.7157° E

Contact: +30 2645 072850

Price Range: €50-€100 per person

Website: sail-lefkas.com

Dining at local tavernas is another opportunity to socialize. I often found myself sharing a table with strangers, exchanging travel stories over a plate of fresh seafood and a glass of local wine.

Solo Activities and Experiences

Lefkada offers plenty of activities that are perfect for solo travelers. One of my favorite solo adventures was hiking the Dimosari Waterfalls. The trail is well-marked and not too challenging, making it ideal for solo hikers. The sense of tranquility as I walked through the forest, listening to the sound of birds and rushing water, was unforgettable.

Another activity I enjoyed was renting a bicycle and exploring the island at my own pace. I rented a bike from "Lefkas Bike Rentals" and spent a day cycling along the coast, stopping at beaches and viewpoints along the way.

Address: Lefkada Town, Lefkada, Greece

Coordinates: 38.8347° N, 20.7001° E

Contact: +30 2645 022750

Price Range: €10-€15 per day

Website: lefkasbikerentals.com

For a more relaxing experience, I took a day trip to Meganisi Island. The ferry ride was scenic, and the island itself was peaceful and less touristy than Lefkada. I spent the day wandering through the small villages and swimming in the crystal-clear waters.

Ferry Port: Nidri, Lefkada, Greece

Coordinates: 38.7167° N, 20.7045° E

Ferry Price: €10-€15 round trip

Reflecting on Your Solo Journey

Traveling solo in Lefkada was an empowering experience. It gave me the freedom to explore at my own pace, make spontaneous decisions, and connect with both the place and myself in a deeper way. Reflecting on my journey, I realized that solo travel isn't just about being alone – it's about discovering who you are and what you truly enjoy.

Lefkada, with its stunning landscapes, welcoming people, and relaxed atmosphere, was the perfect place for this kind of introspective journey. Whether you're a seasoned solo traveler or considering your first solo trip, Lefkada is a destination that will leave you with unforgettable memories and a sense of accomplishment.

Chapter 18

Romantic Getaways – Love in Lefkada

Romantic Beaches and Sunset Spots

Lefkada is nothing short of a paradise for couples seeking a romantic escape. One of the most enchanting experiences on the island is watching the sunset with your loved one at one of its stunning beaches. Picture this: the sun dipping below the horizon, painting the sky with hues of orange, pink, and purple as the gentle waves lap against the shore. This was my experience when I visited Porto Katsiki, a beach renowned not just for its beauty but for the sheer romance it exudes.

Porto Katsiki Beach is located at 38.6003° N, 20.5526° E. The beach itself is a long stretch of white pebbles and sand, with steep cliffs towering behind it. Getting there involves a bit of a trek down a series of stairs, which adds to the anticipation. It's best to arrive in the late afternoon when the crowds have thinned out. The golden hour here is magical, with the sunlight reflecting off the cliffs and the water turning a deep shade of blue. If you're lucky, you might even find a secluded spot just for the two of you.

Opening Hours: Accessible all day

Coordinates: 38.6003° N, 20.5526° E

Address: Porto Katsiki Beach, Lefkada, Greece

Price Range: Free access (Parking fees may apply)

Another spot I'd recommend is Egremni Beach. It's more remote but equally, if not more, beautiful. The journey to this beach can be a bit challenging, especially after the 2015 earthquake that damaged the access road, but the effort is worth it. When you finally reach the beach, you'll be greeted by a pristine stretch of sand and crystal-clear waters. The remoteness of Egremni means it's often less crowded, making it perfect for a romantic escape.

Opening Hours: Accessible all day

Coordinates: 38.6417° N, 20.5675° E

Address: Egremni Beach, Lefkada, Greece

Price Range: Free access (Boat trip fees may apply)

Couples' Resorts and Luxury Stays

When it comes to romantic stays, Lefkada offers a range of luxury resorts that cater to couples. I had the pleasure of staying at the San Nicolas Resort Hotel, which is perched on a hill overlooking the turquoise waters of Mikros Gialos Bay. This resort is ideal for couples looking for privacy and luxury. The rooms are spacious, with large balconies that offer stunning views of the Ionian Sea. What I loved most about this resort was the infinity pool that seemed to merge seamlessly with the sea, offering an unparalleled romantic setting.

San Nicolas Resort Hotel

Opening Hours: Open year-round

Coordinates: 38.6824° N, 20.7186° E

Address: Mikros Gialos, Lefkada, Greece

Phone Number: +30 2645 095310

Price Range: €200 - €500 per night

Website: sannicolas.gr

For those who prefer something even more exclusive, Ionian Blue Hotel is another excellent option. This luxury hotel is located on a hillside and offers panoramic views of the sea. The rooms here are elegantly decorated, and many come with private pools. I found the atmosphere here incredibly serene, perfect for couples wanting to unwind and enjoy each other's company.

Ionian Blue Hotel

Opening Hours: Open year-round

Coordinates: 38.7250° N, 20.6894° E

Address: Nikiana, Lefkada, Greece

Phone Number: +30 2645 092152

Price Range: €150 - €400 per night

Website: ionianblue.gr

Romantic Dinners and Seaside Cafes

Nothing says romance like a candlelit dinner by the sea, and Lefkada has no shortage of romantic dining spots. One evening, I dined at Seaside Restaurant in Vasiliki, a charming little place right by the water's edge. The menu here is a delightful mix of traditional Greek dishes and fresh seafood. I still remember the grilled octopus paired with a crisp glass of white wine. The setting, with the sound of the waves gently lapping the shore, was the perfect backdrop for a romantic evening.

Seaside Restaurant

Opening Hours: 12:00 PM - 11:00 PM

Coordinates: 38.6283° N, 20.6133° E

Address: Vasiliki, Lefkada, Greece

Phone Number: +30 2645 031226

Price Range: €20 - €50 per person

Website: seasidelefkada.gr

If you're looking for something more casual, Rachi Restaurant in the mountain village of Exanthia offers both incredible food and breathtaking views. The restaurant is famous for its sunsets, and it's easy to see why. The sky here turns into a canvas of colors, making it an unforgettable setting for a romantic dinner. I'd recommend trying their traditional Greek dishes, such as moussaka or stuffed peppers, accompanied by a glass of locally produced wine.

Rachi Restaurant

Opening Hours: 5:00 PM - 11:00 PM

Coordinates: 38.7375° N, 20.6197° E

Address: Exanthia, Lefkada, Greece

Phone Number: +30 2645 099059

Price Range: €15 - €40 per person

Website: rachilefkada.com

Activities for Two: Sailing, Spa, and More

One of the most memorable activities I experienced in Lefkada was a private sailing trip around the island. There's something incredibly romantic about being out on the open water with just your partner and the crew. We set sail from the marina in Nidri, exploring hidden coves and secluded beaches that are only accessible by boat. The highlight was anchoring near a small, uninhabited island where we swam in the crystal-clear waters and enjoyed a picnic on the beach.

Opening Hours: Depends on the charter

Coordinates: 38.7048° N, 20.7111° E

Address: Nidri Marina, Lefkada, Greece

Price Range: €300 - €700 for a private charter

Website: nidrisailing.com

For a more relaxing experience, I'd recommend a couple's spa day at the Aroma Dryos Eco & Design Hotel. This luxurious spa offers a range of treatments designed to help you unwind and reconnect. I treated myself to a deep tissue massage, while my partner enjoyed a facial. The spa's serene environment, combined with the expert hands of the therapists, made this an incredibly rejuvenating experience.

Aroma Dryos Eco & Design Hotel

Opening Hours: 10:00 AM - 8:00 PM

Coordinates: 38.7186° N, 20.6836° E

Address: Vasiliki, Lefkada, Greece

Phone Number: +30 2645 097000

Price Range: €50 - €150 per treatment

Website: aromadryos.gr

Honeymooning in Lefkada

Lefkada is an ideal destination for honeymooners, offering a perfect blend of adventure, relaxation, and romance. I've met couples who chose to spend their honeymoon here and raved about the island's charm. One of the key highlights for honeymooners is the variety of experiences available, from exploring the island's natural beauty to indulging in luxurious spa treatments.

Many newlyweds opt to stay in one of the island's boutique hotels, such as the Villa Veneziano. This 18th-century mansion has been converted into a luxury villa with just five suites, each offering a unique blend of traditional charm and modern comfort. The villa's location on a hillside overlooking the sea ensures privacy and stunning views, making it perfect for honeymooners.

Villa Veneziano

Opening Hours: Open year-round

Coordinates: 38.7044° N, 20.7087° E

Address: Perigiali, Lefkada, Greece

Phone Number: +30 2645 097100

Price Range: €250 - €600 per night

Website: villaveneziano.com

Making Memories: Unique Romantic Experiences

Lefkada is full of opportunities to create unique and lasting memories. One of my favorite experiences was a sunset horseback ride along the beach. We booked this through a local stable near Kathisma Beach. Riding along the shore as the sun set, with the waves gently crashing beside us, was an unforgettable experience. The stable offered well-trained horses, and the guide was friendly and knowledgeable, making it a perfect activity for couples.

Opening Hours: 8:00 AM - 8:00 PM

Coordinates: 38.7464° N, 20.6076° E

Address: Kathisma Beach, Lefkada, Greece

Phone Number: +30 2645 095555

Price Range: €50 - €100 per person

Website: lefkadahorses.gr

Another unique experience I'd recommend is taking a cooking class together. We took a class at a small family-run taverna in the village of Karya. The experience of learning to cook traditional Greek dishes, like tzatziki and souvlaki, was not only fun but also gave us skills to recreate a taste of Lefkada back home. The class ended with us enjoying the meal we had prepared together, accompanied by local wine.

Opening Hours: By appointment

Coordinates: 38.7252° N, 20.6319° E

Address: Karya, Lefkada, Greece

Phone Number: +30 2645 091234

Price Range: €50 - €120 per person

Website: cookingclasslefkada.com

Chapter 19

What to Do and What Not to Do – Tips for a Respectful Visit

Cultural Etiquette and Local Customs

Understanding and respecting local customs is crucial when visiting Lefkada. The island has a rich cultural heritage, and locals take pride in their traditions. One of the things I learned quickly is the importance of greetings. When you enter a shop or a taverna, it's polite to greet the staff with a warm "Kalimera" (Good morning) or "Kalispera" (Good evening). This small gesture goes a long way in building rapport with the locals.

Another important custom is respect for religious sites. Lefkada is home to numerous churches and monasteries, many of which are still active places of worship. When visiting these sites, it's important to dress modestly. I made sure to cover my shoulders and knees when I visited the Monastery of Panagia Faneromeni, which is located near the town of Lefkada.

Opening Hours: 8:00 AM - 8:00 PM

Coordinates: 38.8336° N, 20.6947° E

Address: Lefkada, Greece

Phone Number: +30 2645 025273

Price Range: Free entry

Website: faneromenimonastery.gr

How to Dress Appropriately

When it comes to dressing appropriately in Lefkada, it's important to consider both the weather and the setting. The island has a Mediterranean climate, so lightweight, breathable clothing is ideal. However, as I mentioned earlier, when visiting religious sites, it's important to dress modestly. For women, this means covering your shoulders and knees, and for men, it's advisable to avoid wearing shorts.

On the beaches and in the more touristy areas, casual attire is perfectly acceptable. However, if you plan to visit more traditional villages or attend a local event, it's respectful to dress a bit more conservatively. I found that bringing a light scarf or shawl was useful, as it could be easily thrown over my shoulders when needed.

Do's and Don'ts of Dining in Lefkada

Dining in Lefkada is a delight, but there are a few do's and don'ts to keep in mind to ensure you have an authentic and respectful experience. One of the things I quickly learned is that meal times in Greece are different from what I'm used to. Lunch is typically served between 2:00 PM and 4:00 PM, and dinner doesn't usually start until after 8:00 PM. It's also worth noting that tipping is appreciated but not obligatory. I usually left a small tip (around 5-10%) if the service was particularly good.

When dining in a traditional taverna, it's common to share dishes. I loved this aspect of Greek dining because it allowed us to try a variety of dishes without committing to just one. One thing to avoid is asking for ketchup or mayonnaise with your meal. Greek cuisine is flavorful on its own, and adding these condiments is generally frowned upon.

Respecting the Environment: Leave No Trace

Lefkada's natural beauty is one of its greatest assets, and it's crucial to help preserve it for future generations. One of the most important principles to follow when visiting is the "Leave No Trace" principle. This means taking all your rubbish with you when you leave a beach or picnic spot. I made a habit of carrying a small bag with me to collect any litter, and I was pleased to see that most other visitors did the same.

It's also important to stick to marked trails when hiking. The island's ecosystems are delicate, and wandering off the path can damage the flora and fauna. I noticed that many of the popular trails, such as the path to Milos Beach, are well-marked, so it's easy to stay on course.

Opening Hours: Accessible all day

Coordinates: 38.7411° N, 20.6147° E

Address: Lefkada, Greece

Price Range: Free access

Interacting with Locals: How to Be Respectful

Interacting with locals is one of the highlights of visiting Lefkada, but it's important to do so respectfully. I found that learning a few basic Greek phrases went a long way in making connections with the people I met. Even simple words like "Efharisto" (Thank you) and "Parakalo" (Please) were appreciated. The locals are generally friendly and welcoming, but it's important to remember that Lefkada is a small community, and it's best to approach interactions with humility and respect.

One thing I learned is that Greeks value their privacy, so it's important not to be too intrusive. For example, while it's common to see locals sitting outside their homes, it's polite to greet them but avoid prying into their personal lives unless they invite you to do so.

Common Mistakes to Avoid

There are a few common mistakes that I noticed other visitors making during my time in Lefkada, and I'd like to share them so you can avoid them. One of the biggest mistakes is underestimating the sun. Even on a cloudy day, the sun in Lefkada can be intense, so it's essential to wear sunscreen, a hat, and sunglasses. I saw more than a few visitors nursing sunburns because they didn't take proper precautions.

Another mistake is not planning enough time for the island. Lefkada is larger than it appears, and there's so much to see and do. I initially planned to stay for just a few days but ended up extending my stay because there was so much I didn't want to miss. If possible, I'd recommend staying for at least a week to fully experience everything the island has to offer.

Finally, don't make the mistake of sticking only to the tourist hotspots. While places like Porto Katsiki and Nidri are beautiful, some of my favorite experiences were in the quieter, less-visited areas of the island. Take the time to explore the traditional villages, hidden beaches, and local markets—you won't regret it.

Lefkada truly is a gem of the Ionian Sea, offering the perfect blend of romance, adventure, and cultural experiences. Whether you're planning a romantic getaway, a honeymoon, or simply a relaxing vacation, this island has something to offer everyone. With a little preparation and a respectful approach, your time in Lefkada will undoubtedly be an unforgettable experience.

Chapter 20

Practical Information – What You Need to Know

When I first planned my trip to Lefkada, Greece, I knew it was going to be an adventure, but like any seasoned traveler, I wanted to be prepared. There's nothing worse than being caught off guard by small but crucial details that can affect your experience. After spending time on this beautiful island, I've gathered some essential information that I wish someone had told me before I packed my bags. Let me share these with you so your journey is smooth sailing from start to finish.

Currency and Payment Methods

Lefkada, like the rest of Greece, uses the Euro (€) as its official currency. If you're arriving from a country that doesn't use the Euro, it's a good idea to exchange some money before you arrive, although there are plenty of ATMs on the island. I found that most restaurants, shops, and hotels accept credit and debit cards, but cash is still king in smaller villages or for purchasing local crafts and food from markets.

I recommend carrying a mix of cash and cards. You can withdraw Euros from ATMs with most international cards, but be aware of the fees your bank might charge. I was charged a small fee each time I withdrew money, so I made sure to withdraw larger amounts less frequently to avoid multiple charges. The ATMs are mostly concentrated in Lefkada Town and other popular tourist spots, so if you're venturing off the beaten path, make sure you have enough cash on hand.

Language Tips and Useful Phrases

Greek is the official language spoken in Lefkada, and while English is widely understood in tourist areas, a little Greek goes a long way in making connections with locals. I always find that learning a few key phrases in the local language not only enriches the travel experience but also earns you a smile and better service. Here are some basics that came in handy during my stay:

Kaliméra (Καλημέρα) – Good morning

Efcharistó (Ευχαριστώ) – Thank you

Parakaló (Παρακαλώ) – Please / You're welcome

Poso kostízei? (Πόσο κοστίζει;) – How much does it cost?

To logariasmó, parakaló (Το λογαριασμό, παρακαλώ) – The bill, please

You don't need to be fluent, but making the effort to speak a few words in Greek can make a big difference in your interactions. It's also useful to carry a small phrasebook or have a translation app on your phone for those moments when you need a little extra help.

Health and Safety Precautions

Lefkada is generally a safe place to visit, but like anywhere, it's important to take common-sense precautions. During my visit, I found the island to be very welcoming and safe, even when walking around at night. That said, I always recommend sticking to well-lit areas and not leaving valuables unattended, especially on the beaches.

Healthcare on the island is accessible, with a hospital in Lefkada Town and several clinics scattered around. I had a minor incident with a sea urchin while snorkeling, and the care I received at the local clinic was prompt and professional. If you have any specific medical needs, it's wise to bring a supply of your regular medication, as not all prescriptions may be available locally.

For emergencies, dial 112 – this is the general emergency number across the EU. The local hospital is located at 38.8314° N, 20.7089° E.

Lefkada General Hospital

Address: East Lefkada, Lefkada Town, 311 00, Greece

Phone: +30 26450 23900

Website: www.lgh.gr

Emergency Contacts and Services

In an emergency, it's essential to know who to contact and where to go. Aside from the general emergency number 112, here are a few more contacts you might need during your stay:

Police: 100

Fire Department: 199

Ambulance: 166

Tourist Police: +30 26450 29375

I suggest saving these numbers in your phone as soon as you arrive. It's better to be prepared and not need them than to be caught scrambling in a stressful situation.

Communication: SIM Cards and Wi-Fi

Staying connected is important, whether you're navigating your way to a hidden beach or posting envy-inducing photos on Instagram. Most places on Lefkada offer free Wi-Fi, especially in hotels, cafes, and restaurants. However, if you're planning to explore remote areas or want to avoid relying on public Wi-Fi, consider getting a local SIM card.

I picked up a SIM card from one of the many shops in Lefkada Town, and it was a lifesaver. The major carriers are Cosmote, Vodafone, and Wind. Prices are reasonable, and the process is quick – just make sure your phone is unlocked before you travel. A basic prepaid SIM with a few GBs of data cost me around €10, which was more than enough for a week of travel.

If you prefer not to get a local SIM, international roaming might be an option, but be sure to check with your provider about the costs, as they can add up quickly.

Time Zones and Electricity

Lefkada operates on Eastern European Time (EET), which is UTC +2 hours. During daylight saving time, it's UTC +3 hours. This means if you're coming from Western Europe, you'll need to adjust your watch forward by an hour or two. I didn't have any issues with adjusting, but it's something to keep in mind, especially if you're booking transportation or tours.

Electricity in Greece runs on 230V with a frequency of 50Hz, and the plugs are type C and F. If you're coming from the UK, the US, or other countries with different plug types, make sure to bring an adapter. I always carry a universal travel adapter with multiple USB ports, which came in handy for charging all my devices at once.

Travel Insurance: Do You Need It?

I can't stress enough the importance of travel insurance. You never know what might happen on your trip, and having insurance can save you from a lot of stress and expense. From flight cancellations to medical emergencies, travel insurance covers a range of unexpected situations.

I've been in situations where I had to cancel part of my trip due to illness, and my travel insurance was a lifesaver, covering the costs I would have otherwise lost. When traveling to Lefkada, or anywhere else for that matter, make sure your insurance policy covers the basics – medical emergencies, trip cancellations, lost luggage, and any specific activities you plan to do, like diving or sailing.

It's worth spending a little extra for comprehensive coverage. Check with your provider before you go and keep a copy of your policy and emergency contact numbers with you at all times.

Appendix

Additional Resources for Your Trip

As your journey through Lefkada unfolds, having a few extra resources at your fingertips can make a world of difference. Here's a handy appendix filled with useful information that might come in handy during your stay.

A. Emergency Contacts

Police: 100

Fire Department: 199

Ambulance: 166

Tourist Police: +30 26450 29375

Lefkada General Hospital:

Address: East Lefkada, Lefkada Town, 311 00, Greece

Phone: +30 26450 23900

Website: www.lgh.gr

B. Maps and Navigational Tools

I found Google Maps to be incredibly useful for getting around Lefkada, but there are also several good offline maps you can download before you arrive. I used Maps.me, which allowed me to navigate even when I didn't have cell service. For hiking and exploring off the beaten path, consider getting a physical map from a local bookstore in Lefkada Town.

Map of Lefkada

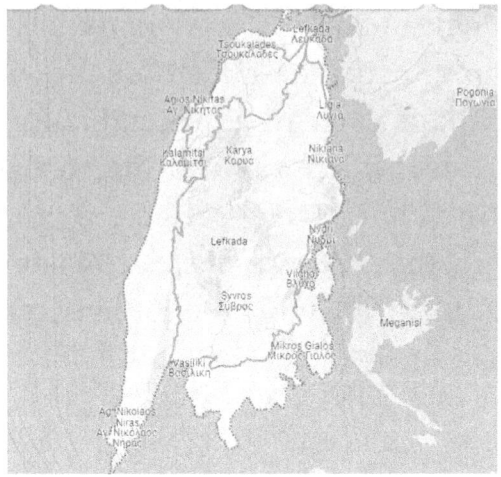

https://maps.app.goo.gl/AjREUZuyxs9YuxE9A

SCAN THE IMAGE/QR CODE WITH YOUR PHONE TO GET
THE LOCATIONS IN REAL TIME

Map of things to do in Lefkada

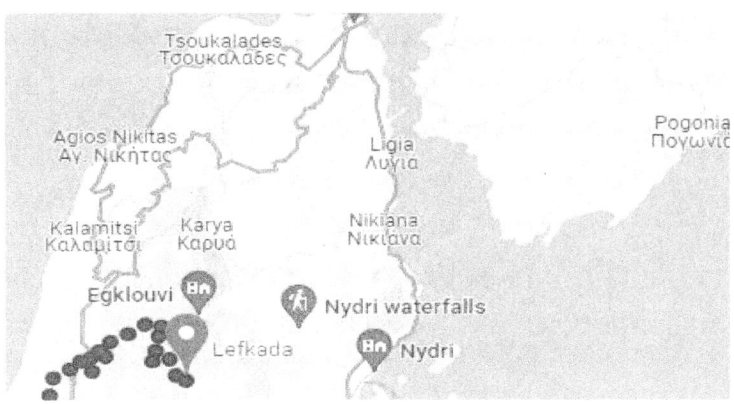

https://www.google.com/maps/search/Things+to+do/@38.7070233,20.4722274,11z/data=!3m1!4b1!4m7!2m6!3m5!2sLefkada!3s0x135db414da08c147:0x949e9819e6f840c6!4m2!1d20.64073!2d38.7066464?entry=ttu

SCAN THE IMAGE/QR CODE WITH YOUR PHONE TO GET THE LOCATIONS IN REAL TIME

C. Additional Reading and References

For those who want to delve deeper into the history and culture of Lefkada, here are some books I found informative and enjoyable:

"Lefkada: The Island of Poets and Seafarers" by Nikos Athanassopoulos

"Lefkada: A Complete Guide to the Island" by Dimitris Kosmas

"The Ionian Islands" by John Freely

D. Useful Local Phrases

Kaliméra (Καλημέρα) – Good morning

Efcharistó (Ευχαριστώ) – Thank you

Parakaló (Παρακαλώ) – Please / You're welcome

Poso kostízei? (Πόσο κοστίζει;) – How much does it cost?

To logariasmó, parakaló (Το λογαριασμό, παρακαλώ) – The bill, please

E. Addresses and Locations of Popular Accommodation

Porto Galini Seaside Resort & Spa

Address: Nikiana, Lefkada, 311 00, Greece

Phone: +30 26450 92350

Price Range: €150-€300/night

Website: www.portogalini.gr

Ionian Blue Hotel

Address: Nikiana, Lefkada, 311 00, Greece

Phone: +30 26450 29029

Price Range: €120-€250/night

Website: www.ionianblue.gr

F. Addresses and Locations of Popular Restaurants and Cafes

Thymari

Address: 6 Antoniou Valaoritou, Lefkada Town, 311 00, Greece

Phone: +30 26450 22900

Price Range: €20-€40 per person

Opening Hours: 12:00 PM - 11:00 PM

Taverna Ionio

Address: Agios Nikitas, Lefkada, 311 00, Greece

Phone: +30 26450 97273

Price Range: €15-€30 per person

Opening Hours: 11:00 AM - 10:00 PM

G. Addresses and Locations of Popular Bars and Clubs

Lighthouse

Address: Frini, Lefkada Town, 311 00, Greece

Phone: +30 26450 21610

Price Range: €8-€15 per drink

Opening Hours: 9:00 PM - 4:00 AM

Baccara Cocktail Bar

Address: Lefkada Town, 311 00, Greece

Phone: +30 26450 22200

Price Range: €10-€20 per drink

Opening Hours: 7:00 PM - 3:00 AM

H. Addresses and Locations of Top Attractions

Porto Katsiki Beach

Coordinates: 38.6020° N, 20.5506° E

Address: West Coast of Lefkada, Greece

Opening Hours: Accessible all day

Price Range: Free entry

Egremni Beach

Coordinates: 38.6191° N, 20.5522° E

Address: West Coast of Lefkada, Greece

Opening Hours: Accessible all day

Price Range: Free entry

I. Addresses and Locations of Book Shops

Evdokia's Books

Address: 3 Ioannou Mela, Lefkada Town, 311 00, Greece

Phone: +30 26450 21005

Opening Hours: 9:00 AM - 8:00 PM

Veranda Bookstore

Address: 12 Fotomara, Lefkada Town, 311 00, Greece

Phone: +30 26450 21255

Opening Hours: 10:00 AM - 7:00 PM

J. Addresses and Locations of Top Clinics, Hospitals, and Pharmacies

Lefkada General Hospital

Address: East Lefkada, Lefkada Town, 311 00, Greece

Phone: +30 26450 23900

Website: www.lgh.gr

Pharmacy Savva Kosta

Address: 10 Ioannou Mela, Lefkada Town, 311 00, Greece

Phone: +30 26450 21630

Opening Hours: 8:00 AM - 9:00 PM

K. Addresses and Locations of UNESCO World Heritage Sites

While Lefkada itself doesn't have any UNESCO World Heritage Sites, nearby Corfu does. If you're planning a day trip or an extended stay in the region, consider visiting:

Old Town of Corfu

Coordinates: 39.6236° N, 19.9215° E

Address: Corfu Town, Corfu, Greece

Opening Hours: Accessible all day

Price Range: Free entry

Photo/Image Attribute

https://commons.wikimedia.org/wiki/File:Kiteboarding_Cape_Verde.jpg

https://commons.wikimedia.org/wiki/File:Egremni_beach_SF_0004.jpg

https://commons.wikimedia.org/wiki/File:Agios_Nikolaos_R02.jpg

https://www.freepik.com/free-photo/lentil-soup-with-mixed-ingredients-herbs-white-bowl-with-spoon_5587973.htm#fromView=search&page=1&position=20&uuid=b684e640-cd16-4ce3-b2ed-4218566017a0

https://www.freepik.com/free-photo/moored-yachts-stand-port-town_6059621.htm#fromView=search&page=3&position=13&uuid=06f7cc72-4ab1-49ea-b6e9-296f313010af

https://www.freepik.com/free-photo/aerial-shot-dock-with-many-boats-docked-water_7848697.htm#fromView=search&page=3&position=12&uuid=06f7cc72-4ab1-49ea-b6e9-296f313010af

Printed in Great Britain
by Amazon

48436466R00126